EXISTENTIAL DIALOGUES

By

Daniel Chechick

Translated from Hebrew by Zvi Chazanov

"We must believe in free will - we have no other choice."

Isaac Bashevis Singer

Table of Contents

Prologue

◆ ◆ ◆

My dear Readers whom I've just met! Let me begin with revealing to you a secret: I intended to make myself null and void. I almost leaped towards the Great Beyond, from the great rocks down the supposedly sure abyss. Yet something kept me back at the very last moment. If it wasn't for that stop, many would have been wandering now how come that young man drew the final curtain on his Play of Life at such an early scene, having experienced none of the climaxes had in store for him. Yet little did they know that my soul had already taken more than the common share of existential questions preoccupying my world since my damned infancy.

These uneasy moments seemed to go forever, in a perpetual war between my desire to live and my desire to annul myself. Let me also reveal to you that this horror had possessed me like some divine decree, but then, in a uniquely miraculous manner, I conceived a magic, entirely surprising solution. It was - starting to converse with myself, following Descartes, who, by doubting everything, erased, in a way, all human lore accumulated until then, to rethink about everything ex nihilo, drawing from his own mind alone!

But then I deemed talking with myself will not suffice, realizing that I am confined within the bounds of my own knowledge, so I needed a counterpart to challenge my ideas and quench my awful curiosity reflected in my great questions. But who could that person be? After all, the only one around here was myself, and it's highly unacceptable to talk to yourself, or others might deem you insane. To handle this difficulty, I conceived a magical, though somewhat childish solution, which I guess you too, dear readers, resort to very often. I decided to pretend I am two persons conversing, one being a sage sharing his lifelong-acquired wisdom in the twilight of his life.

Since we all accept any solution, which cheers up human hearts, let us delve right away into my inner dialogues with my other personality, who is nothing but a slight variation of myself. Yes, I know it sounds confusing, but I also know you indulge in it as well, so dealing with an issue together brings us together. Thus, my dialogues with myself resemble the silent dialogues we all have with ourselves before falling asleep, when facing a magnificent outdoor landscape, and even during the all too familiar moments of melancholy and solitude. No matter how mightily enchanted with your own reality you might be, I suppose you too happened to deliberate certain decisions with your inner self.

In a moment, I lay my soul down completely exposed to you, presenting all my emotions so openly you could judge every possible aspect of me. Therefore, let me tell you my psyche juggles between the awful and the wonderful, in my private world where no thought is too blatant, no love is too secret, no anxiety is too abominable and no smile is too vicious to be brought to mind. In a moment, you'll find out your Play of Life is an unprecedented, wonderful masterpiece, so even if you are doubtful in this regard, just accept it as an extraordinary compliment.

Chapter One:
RECALLING MOM'S OR DAD'S LOOKS

◆ ◆ ◆

O nce in a while, I indulge in prophecies about my thoughts and emotions in my old age, and then I'm overwhelmed with horrible anxieties which my reason strives to suppress completely. It puzzles me.

Go ahead; feel absolutely free to share it with me!

On those occasions, I envision myself as one of those godforsaken souls whose outrageous fortune doomed them to spend the rest of their lives in complete solitude. Those people are buried in their daily routine of a morning walk to their benches in the park, as long as their legs didn't give way, where they are engulfed with that cruel silence, which afflicts those who have nobody to have a word with. Such a person, in order to escape humiliation by one's own consciousness, doesn't even dare to express one's thoughts aloud, lest those overhearing him deem him or her insane.

Why are you afraid of becoming as forsaken as him? How likely is this to come true?

Of course, I have no rational reason to feel this way, but what human fears and anxieties are rational, after all? My thoughts are just carried to that realm of unlikely catastrophe, with which I struggle. Nonetheless, I beg you to listen to my subtle words.

My Sincerest apologies. Please, go on.

Well, I am afraid I might outlive everybody else, and be the last to perish, after I have witnessed the life stories of them all, with nobody to appreciate my own. Do you see my point?

Your, existential reality, so excitingly expressed, had kindled my heart, since all humans share this fear, though every individual articulates it differently. Isn't this the greatest and deepest of all human fears?

What is the Great Play of Life all about when the audience has gone!? After all, you are certainly an unworthy audience of your own play! So here you are, imagining a situation where you have nobody to trigger your emotions, with reminders like: as a child, you did so and so..., to the extent of you doubting your own past, having nobody to attest to it.

You read my mind precisely! It is a tremendous horrifying, to outlive your acquaintances. I cannot decide which of my two old-age fears haunts me worse: either this one, or the inability even to envision the faces of my mother and father, or other loved ones.

This fear is nothing but a way of suppressing the recognition of your own mortality, in the form of imagining the loss of members of your circle. After all, their existence served you, inadvertently, to conceal the all too common fear of finiteness, so their absence probably forced you to face this inevitability sooner than you probably liked to. But, look how wonderful is the trick your psyche played, how cunningly our mind is manipulated. Or, if you wish to put it this way, the manipulation one exerts on one's psyche. Isn't it a revolutionary approach?

Hold it! Do you suggest that all these thoughts actually express the fear of my own perish?!

Correct. As natural your feelings about your own death might be, one's courage is attested by the capacity of accepting the Absence of Life. After all, reality allows nothing like Death, just an Absence of Life. Since so far we have no definite knowledge of what happens after one's demise, we cannot assume the dead "go somewhere". All we know is that their life as we knew them ceased. This complex concept allows humans to overcome their fears of their own finiteness, realizing that one will not be there to experience one's last moment. In other words, one realizes we could not know we had already departed. There is a reason why one only sees one's the death of fellow-human's, but finds it hard to contemplate one's own death. I am perfectly aware of this psychological approach being beyond the understanding of most mortals. Therefore, I wish you to reiterate this statement in your mind.

Does it mean that all my thoughts about the inevitable end of my loved ones are nothing but worries about my own loss? Your approach seems unconceivably egocentric, since my boundless and unconditional love for my dear ones is beyond any doubt. Yet I do understand the rigorous analytic logic which drove you to say what you've just said. It compels me to recognize my own finiteness, which, in turn, will also illustrate to me the finiteness of others as well.

But what did you mean by saying that one manipulates one's own mind? Isn't it the other way around?

I have no certain knowledge of that. However, I believe that psyche cannot be perceived as completely isolated from the individual. Rather, it's the individual's metaphoric and delusional intellect that manipulates psyche. Thus, if you have some anxiety, all your manipulations serve to conceal your vulnerabilities. However, such reasoning is possible for an adult who seek defenses, but how could it be managed by an infant suppressing a traumatic experience, which emerges in adulthood? How could the child's[1] infant brain manage to protect him at such an early age? How did his brain know this was the right thing to do? How did it realize that such an experience threatens the person's peace of mind?

I, like the Greek philosophers, failed to crack this enigma, of the balance of powers between human psyche and human intellect.

---

[1] Sometimes, a child exposed to extreme experiences such as domestic violence of grave danger may surprisingly repress them until adulthood. This capacity is yet to be explained. But an even more amazing mental capacity is that of reliving the event in dreams, once the mind is capable of dealing with such horrible memories.

As far as the human that is me is concerned, I am certain than my intellect works in less than full capacity, since my psyche is infested with fears and anxieties, which restricts my existence. However, if I was fortunate enough to listen to the conclusions of your intellect, which dare probe even to depth the of the psyche, this would have been a real life-transforming miracle.

How would you like the audience to appreciate your Play of Life?

Chapter Two:
ON DESPAIR

◆ ◆ ◆

There are those days, when my whole world turns grey, so grey that not even a beautiful child's smile can reach for my soul through that wall of bleakness. Such days compel to withdraw into myself, seeking refuge from melancholy, when I struggle with the despair all around me that leaves no way out.

Some days are so grey by nature they can carry you to the abyss of despair and melancholy.

This may be the reason why all those stormy climes produced so many authors of sublime and universally admired works of art. Those artists simply sought refuge from the effects of the outside world in the privacy of their rooms, where they resigned to their Muse.

What about you? Could you escape from the outer darkness into your inner light?

I am amazed at your assumption, that I might possess some inner light. After all, one is not very familiar with one's own inner light.

There is an abundance of light in you, yet some forces resist your growth and enhance your despair.

Well, then, how can I escape despair?

Let me tell you a little story. Many years ago, when I traveled to New Zealand, I saw a tree that really amazed me: it didn't look special, yet it stood all alone on a lakebed. I suppose that as a younger tree, it had send roots in the land when it was dry, before the great waters drowned it, leaving it overwhelmed with yearning for sunlight. Yet even this condition didn't drive it to despair and die, but made it blossom, bringing love and happiness to all the people who visit it. It inspired them with their own inner powers which, far from being limited, always surprise them.

I reckon Nature can provide us with the noblest arguments for believing in recovery and resurrection into perpetual growth out of destruction.

However, sadly enough, human minds find it difficult to absorb this lesson, preferring to succumb to their grim contemplations. But long practice can imprint this concept in one's mind, make one memorize it like some mantra: even when darkness seems to invade and overwhelm you completely, you can still lit your infinite light which will re-create your world, once you choose to.

If this subtle parable isn't clear enough, one may look into the hearts of those who lost all the world they had known in horrible wars, which sometimes left them all alone in this world. Perhaps they, just like that lonesome tree, resolved to fight on, building a new world from their mind's ruins. can a desperate person absorb this plain lesson?

In other words, even in the abyss of horror, humans have a choice. From here follows one's own terrible responsibility for becoming whatever one desires to. If one is currently desperate, let one engage in a one's soul-searching to find out what sustains despair in one's mind, or, conversely, one's hidden benefits from despair.

My own experience taught me that sometimes, being stuck offers a great defense, like some inner voluntary imprisonment protecting us from discovering what might be a better alternative, as well as from reaching the terrible conclusion that all our long inner imprisonment was just a waste of time.

I found it very painful to hear.

Why?

Because the magic power of words can sometimes generate in us a powerful awareness that you must handle, which, in turn, generates gigantic transformations of your mind. This intellectual penitence might be a source of great pain, but also of an inspiration to discover one's strongest energies. All this generates the metamorphosis leading you to make a choice and reclaim control of your life.

The history of humankind is full of evidence to moments of existential darkness, when humans were robbed of any control of their lives. Yet even then, champions of freedom emerged, fighting to the bitter end, preferring to die proudly rather than lose their grip on their lives, since you can take everything from humans, except their domination of their own minds.

Even in such all-engulfing horror, you can see people living a life that is meaningful, and such a lesson should sink in the contemporary desperate souls as well.

Our dialogue's conclusion can inspire even a desperate person to shake of his despair!

Everyone who is in one's inner prison, should address, at a moment of sincerity, these questions: How long will you remain locked up? Will you ever muster enough courage to break out? The key to your prison is right inside you!

Chapter Three:
FACING HUMANITY

◆ ◆ ◆

Let's take a walk along the main streets, to get infatuated by all kinds of faces and looks!

What do you mean?

I love to look at human faces.

To what purpose?

A very good question...honestly speaking, I fancy myself as my idol, Sherlock Holmes, enquiring into the faces of passers-by as if they are forensic evidence, in an attempt to retrace their biographies, speculating how they looked as infants, and reconstructing their live trajectories, step-by-step. Don't you find it fascinating?

How presumptuous of you, to analyze their lives backwards, in an attempt to figure out their very beginning! It is as if you try to predict the past, while usually one only predicts the future, and I wonder which attempt is more erroneous. However, what traits did you detect in those passers-by?

Some I found vulgar, while others I found subtle and yet others wonderfully peculiar. I saw shattered dreams, great romances and weeping eyes. Eyes infatuate me easily, as you know...

Why?

It's strange, and I suppose that even Darwin was amazed at this human quality: eyes are the windows of the soul, which reveal all its secret. So I just look at them and read those secrets, of joys and sorrows, loves and concealed passions. Though I cannot confirm or disprove what I read in them, they fascinated me as if they are hard facts. This is what infatuates me.

I am amazed at your ability to stop in your tracks, and just look. I miss this ability passionately.

Moreover, when I observe people, I fancy myself a gifted painter, who can picture the wealthy as lonely and godforsaken poor.

Why?

This serendipity just necessitates it, and it involves a great skill of appreciation. Once the arrogant rich gentleman poses for a portrait, I draw him as a godforsaken and lost to the world.

Once I hand him the portrait, he rages, crying this was not what he had asked for. I give away this mental portrait free, begging for his pardon, remarking,

"This will teach you to appreciate your present state. Remember that the frivolous hand of Chance could have begotten you born, or driven you to choose otherwise, to make you resemble this portrait. So smile at the present, love and give, taking nothing for granted!"

Once his shock at my words subsides, his eyes will probably betray his agreement, even if his tongue will be too proud to express it. Yet I'll proud myself for touching his heart.

You are clever and yet insolent, since you cannot force your insights on others. But, lo and behold, you have managed to miraculously transform an arrogant person - supposedly with no intention to – through an imaginary picture!

Correct. After all, I have outlived embarrassment already, being at the end of the road, with contemplations to share, and with no need of favors. Maybe one is allowed a couple of philosophical excesses, since there are no reviews after one's Play of Life final curtain.

How wicked you can be! How could I have judged you so hastily!

Why do you say so?

Because I forgot all this only happens in your mind...yet what an enchanting idea!

So what do you, readers, detect in the eyes of others?

Chapter Four:
BEING INSANE. THAT IS, JUST BEING.

◆ ◆ ◆

Once, I deemed myself as one barred from Truth, as if I was mentally retarded or mentally disordered. Although I was treated, seemingly, like a normal person, I was barred from the secrets shared by all the people around me.

Look at that charming loony fellow walking by the café, completely oblivious of his condition. I envy him, I really do: he's just happy, thanks to the absence of that existential anxiety which controls my world. How can I become like him? How can I shake off my meaningless world, which keeps me alive? Oh dear, what fears haunt me! After all, I don't really wish to annihilate myself. That is, I lack the courage it takes. So here I am, haunted by vicious suspicions of that fellow being just a pretender, or a wizard who managed to break out of our mundane banality, turning his life into poetry, romancing leafless trees and getting engaged in all those bizarre actions which makes him smile incessantly. At certain moments, he can stare straight into your eyes without a blink, as if reading your mind, with that never-changing look...He makes me choke with embarrassment, feeling utterly exposed. Then, he devilishly surprises me with a childish smile, such that I am no longer capable of generating!

what business do you have becoming insane? Aren't you one already?

Sometimes it seems so, indeed! Once he gave me that look, I was dominated by fear, unable to control myself no longer, realizing I am just a bunch of weaknesses merely struggling to survive.

Welcome to the club! In fact, most of us are insane, and since this insanity is so common, it is no longer condemned. However, bear in mind that a whole personality must contain an ounce of madness, a touch of loony-ness, or else that person could not survive one's life.

It is a reassurance to know I am not alone in this struggle, that people share my unsettling sensations. I can even viciously smile at the fact that others suffer just as hard as I do. It means they are living things, rather than some puppets with fake smiles. I hope you don't deem this feeling of mine too sinister.

You must never feel bad about it: it is a great solace to belong to something, to have a sort of loving home like the one you remember you had long ago. Well, thanks to his extraordinary audacity, that lunatic just feels at home all the time, feeling free to dance as if nobody's watching him, sing out loud and bloom right in front of our very eyes, which pop out of their sockets with jealously. His life is the self-fulfillment we all yearn for, the epitome of living free and, most importantly, feeling free every single moment, shaking off our mind-forged and heart-forged manacles which confine us. So tell me, you young at heart, do you know how to reach his insanity? Mind you, hallucinatory substances frighten me, and in addition, the joy and relaxation they promise are more ephemeral than we wish them to be.

Well, I don't have any perfect solution, since if I had I would've made a fortune by selling it to the whole world. Nonetheless, worry not, my friend, I won't leave you empty handed. I plan to go insane only where I feel at home to; where I can express and experience my full-blown spirit; I can

be compared to an introvert violinist, who lies low in most fields of life, yet suddenly explodes with musical of creativity, he senses the full splendor and magnificence of one's mad love for Life, grimacing beyond control, as if transforming himself into some concerto. Maybe it's you who enchant my imagination, with the universes you create in the minds of the young eager for your wisdom and guidance. Maybe you have gone insane as well, through your passion for life...what is most wonderful, is that those handful of mad moments become everything to us, equating us to the really insane we have always dreamt of becoming, and those minutes outlast and overshadow the rest of our lives, when we only wish for that insanity.

Such a secret can indeed drive you insane: bear in mind, that such magic moments infuse your world with the mysterious wonders of being, suppressing all damned conflicts of our lives.

So how does your own peculiar insanity manifest itself?

Chapter Five:
WHAT WRINKLES MEAN

◆ ◆ ◆

My consciousness is manacled by mundane existence: I'm like a child who all of a sudden realizes one's damn finiteness, and from now on has to cope with that unbearable reality of Time as a life imprisonment without parole. Yet my imagination entertains the possibility of escaping the sentence of my intellect, returning to being and acting like the child I used to be, who believed himself to be a child forever...

Honestly speaking, you must admit that the only thing keeping you from

becoming whoever you wish to be is you!

Yet, how could I become a child again? Look at me! Can't you see the encroaching wrinkles around my blue eyes?...

...And it all happened unnoticed by me at all, as early as my very twenties! You cannot imagine how I felt once I realized that: here I am, smiling mindlessly, while my face is growing wrinkled like some ancient relic, resembling your face. And here's the worst of it: I cannot conceal it any longer!

Once my childhood friends see me, they inevitably will regard my face as the evidence of the long time passing, and I'll immediately break down, retreating to the wonderland of self-deluding denial.

I know how you feel, since our greatest fear is the fear of truth in the first moments after it is revealed. It is only natural of you to deny and denounce your body, as if it belonged to another entity. However, what marvels me is that as time goes by, with you gaining more outward attributes aging, you grow accustomed to them and even consider it a great privilege to be marked with wrinkles all over.

God forbid assuming I am appalled by own wrinkles, and, consequently, by those on your face. It's just that all my life I had believed this can only happen to other people, and suddenly, in some miraculously inexplicable manner, it happened to me too, so my mind is in a terrible turmoil.

It is inevitable, like our casting in the Play of Life: some play the younger ones, while others, the older ones. Yet, although the cast replacement never ceases, once we face it we are utterly shocked. But keep up hope, and see in how many ways such a wrinkled rag of my age can bring out his Inner Child. It's all up to us. One who feels comfortable about succumbing to the notion of finiteness, actually decides not to unleash one's Inner Child. Would you believe that?

Sometimes, making a choice is the greatest challenge life throws at you.

One might love one's submission to conventions one chooses to regard as "problems", rather than challenges or missions in life, which might inspire a person with a resolution to tackle them. You should better ask yourself why you make such choices, since, whether you like it or not, you cannot defy the very fact of finiteness, and you're bound to change with time. Now, you can only choose how to face the world, by looking at its bright side or dark side. This is the decision your soul must make. It is absolutely up to you to choose to play the hero or the victim in your life's drama.

Therefore, always remember that you can choose to be enchanted with your reality at every single moment of your life. Regardless of how short-lived, subtle and minor this enchantment may be, it will nonetheless stir your blood. By some magic law of the universe, there are endless varieties of these enchantments. That is to say, both the young, and even the old and wrinkled ones, have countless ways to enjoy their Play of Life. Even the very old ones can still get intoxicated with the scent of Youth and feel excited until they draw their very last breath! Can anything more inspiring than the sight of an old and wrinkled smile?

Perfectly correct! This conversation will be engraved on my mind, just as the imperative to always keep my world smiling!

So what do you feel at the sight of others' wrinkles?

Chapter Six:
MASTERING THE ART OF ERRING

◆ ◆ ◆

Upon examining the course of my life, it first seemed nothing but an amazing sequence of terrible errors. Yet currently, 1 can hardly regard them as errors at all, but rather opportunities to realize my potential, occurring due to my admirable ability to make choices. How should we regard those wonderful parents who teach their children how to err? How can making mistakes be the right thing?

Yet this is not the case. Errors are manifestations of revolutionary thinking, stemming from highly individualistic, subjectivist philosophy. Errors offer you a wonderful life. My dear mother kept telling me that you get no reviews at the end of your Play of Life. From here follows that one must indulge in life to extremes, until one feels his or her soul is infused with awe and greatness and one is infatuated with one's reality, accepting one's flaws as well as one's unperceivable perfection.

Yet only few bother to master the art of erring, right? Since infancy, I was instructed to succumb to social standards and natural necessities, and accomplish required achievements. Our companions, teachers and judges incessantly measuring and grading our worth. Therefore I, as a product of this society, grew up to be just another social grades hunter, tormenting myself, for every single mistake I made, with misgivings, anxieties, and frustration, which are so popular in this psychoactive-drug-addicted world of ours. If it wasn't for the drugs, I would've succumbed to melancholy lurking in the back of my mind.

I guess the rat race you've just described offers no comfort, thus driving humans to sacrifice themselves to socialization. Yet our souls, nearly crushed to perdition by society, muster all their strength, amidst all the storm of mad howling, to implore us, in a most subtle way: "can't you see your real desires that occupy your hearts and minds? Yes, you are capable of following them, if you just make your true choices!".

Yet humans brutally suppress the attempts of their souls to save them from themselves. This brutal struggle can never cease until, in some miraculous way, one starts erring, that is, living a really human life!

You demand too much of humankind, such as to start living a real life, or follow our natural capacities. However, it is inevitable that only few could resign to their true desires and pay the terrible price for their choices. What if their choices are more than just socially unacceptable, but may also abhor their loved ones? How can one be true to oneself and live a full life in such a confining world?

my dear friend, the road to living sincerely is long and rugged. Being your true self is modern humankind's greatest challenge, with all forces of reality fighting your rebellious attempt at choosing the way truest to yourself.

Lets us make a momentous intellectual endeavor, asking ourselves whether we regard each and every one of our loved ones as a wonderfully unique, unprecedented world, as an unparalleled, individual mind inhabited by conflicting and contradicting emotions which only that individual can sense. Can we perceive that individual as one with dark and sinister desires generating one's blatant and so unbearable downsides? Do we really see the person in front of us as an individual dealing with all kinds of existential questions? Or, maybe we only perceive other people's relation to ourselves? This, my friend, is the greatest question which we practically cannot deal with in this alienated world, where one must always fit in the right box, while those choosing to follow their innermost desires are doomed to be tormented for and by their choices, and even torment their loved ones. So which is the best way of life? What is life with no errors?! What kind of a human can always succumb to standard demands, never breaking away and living out the life we can only live once?

Let's go back to our intellectual experiment where we expose our vulnerabilities. Let us imagine the person we've described, that inconceivable assembly of contradictions, facing us. Suddenly, we welcome him with a sympathetic embrace, which drives home to him that we, just like him, are both horrible and wonderful beings, and therefore understand him; that we, too, face life with the same fears and resolution. Thus we demonstrate to him that we, too, resort to numerous contradictory strategies, in an attempt to act out our Play of Life with all its infinite complexity. Only such a perception allows us to see a person as a whole instead of messing around with his or her undesirable components. Such a perception allows a person to regard his errors as a part of a Play of Life, both universal and peculiar at the same time - an attitude this judgmental and categorizing world of ours needs so desperately.

From this so uncommon perception follows, that the best thing one can wish for is an extraordinary and faithful partner to act with him that wonderful Play of Life. Such a partner should share his unique existential conflict like a blood brother, without whom none of them could have survived this world and realize that despite their existential attachment, which is selfless love rather than a selfish interest, each of them still bears the ultimate responsibility for one's Play of Life, with all its errors.

Honestly speaking, I wonder whether your utopian philosophy is ever practiced, since such a utopia only exists in some secluded hermitages. After all, we cannot really handle the darkest abysses of our fellow-humans' minds, and perhaps we are not especially enthusiastic about exploring them, so we just suppress this reality. Yet how wonderful it feels to know that one is entirely transparent to one's fellow-humans, who accept him with boundless love free of denial and suppression, and are fully aware of one's existential struggle, regardless of one's actions of choices. Such acceptance as you referred to, takes unconditional, undeserved love, like a mother's love for her children.

Sometimes, unconditional love seems like a mission impossible, but one must never give up trying, since one is driven to it, mostly by one's human sensitivity and empathy. Such love fascinates us even more than life, since the most sublime happiness for a human is to be as loved as a newborn.

How strong is your fear of errors?

Chapter Seven:
EVERYMAN'S INNER FIGHT

◆ ◆ ◆

I guess you are familiar with that feeling, when at some moment in your life, after you had already seen a thing or two and established your convictions—all of a sudden you happen to see a baby-cart with a creature of marvelous beauty in it, sleeping, engulfed with such an enchantingly mighty bliss. It may not even be fully conscious of its very existence, enchanted by some existential hallucination. Trying, in vain, to imagine yourself in his condition, you conclude you have never been like that. This gives you a sense of powerlessness, driving home to you that Time has usurped control over your entire life. So you just look at that baby, wondering what course the rest of its life will take, and through what milestones. This unwillingly drives me to envision myself under entirely different circumstances: somewhere in the far future, I participate in a fantastic and top- secret experiment, where expert "soul-catching" offered me the following deal: they will infuse my soul in a newborn, on one critical condition - that I will relive my whole life exactly as I have been living it so far.

To my question, they insisted that indeed, I must relive my whole life, with all their moments of charm and horror.
Upon, hearing this, I remained breathless, seeing in front of me my whole childhood and adolescence, with all my own and my family's moments of horrors, my innocence, exploding curiosity, experiences, romances, and perils I went through, all the way to my recent years of wonder. So now, they want me to answer immediately whether I am willing to relive my whole past all over again. How can I muster the mental strength it takes!?

Beware of such offers, they might expand your consciousness infinitely! Most of the people I know have already lived their lives to the full, and I suspect very few of them will accept the offer of those soul-catching illustrious scholars. It is common knowledge that a human life has an abundance of certain experiences, which overshadow the moments of happiness, so one cannot blame them for their unwillingness to experience the very lives they had all over again.

Forget about them, Buddy! What about me? I have just embarked on my life's journey, building up myself. Look what experiences inhabit my world! Why is it that in my world, too, Darkness overpower Light? Shouldn't my youthful optimism make it the other way around? How could have I allowed it?! How dare I not stand up and proudly declare that my life deserves reliving? And if my life so far deserve it not, what is meant by viewing my future life?

You are to be blamed neither for the hardships in your life nor for it being miserable compared to others' lives. After all, what are your hardships and miseries but manifestations of the magnificent elements which made you what you are?

See what a wonderful moral we can derive from your question! If most people are reluctant to experience their lives once again, it means they had lived through some extremely unpleasant experiences, indelibly impressed upon their fragile minds. This is to say that every one of us lives through endless inner fight, unnoticed even by one's closest circle.

Meanwhile we, the outside observers, pass judgment on our fellow-humans despite our total ignorance of their lives, waiving the rules of elementary decency. We base our judgment on trifle details, unaware of how terribly little of the Big Picture we see. Our view of the lives of others is distorted, because we examine them through a telescope aimed at a single, accidental, usually insignificant spot, thus disregarding the entire world outside the lens.

On the other hand, look how emphatic one becomes thanks to this awareness to this mental inner fight within all of us humans. Just imagine what an explosion of kindness it can trigger, and how it can diametrically transform our perception of life from alienation to sensitive and containing embrace! Can you realize just how humane we can grow, far beyond what we had ever imagined? All it takes is just us imagining our fellow-human lamenting one's life at a certain moment, and lo and behold, we regard that fellow favorably, rather than negatively, even if we hardly know him or her! What an intellectual miracle with a universal humane lesson it is!

Just as I hoped, you demonstrated once again how can Light overcome Darkness!

Would you agree to relive your lives, exactly as you have lived them so far, with all their brightest and darkest sides?

Chapter Eight:
I WANT TO RESEMBLE "THEM" A LITTLE

◆ ◆ ◆

Occasionally, I fancy myself one of "them", those wonderfully carefree people, outside this room, whose senseless smiles never seem to stop. I mean all the people who are not me. As you can observe, those who neither draw any conclusions, nor are tormented by existential horrors, collapse under life's hardships, nor scorched by mundane existence. Instead, they just live happily. Sometimes I believe they just live from one event to the next one with blissful indifference, welcoming every event with a smile. So where am I, compared to them? Why do my contemplations keep haunting me, and my mind suppresses my pleasure? Why do I always have to assess future risks and anticipate my future emotions, while all those people seem to enjoy the moment, leading a life which is sincere and, most importantly, uncomplicated? Suppose I become like them for a moment - could I have any fun at that moment, or at any moment of my life?

I guess you, intellectuals and philosophically oriented chose, either intentionally or unintentionally, to live another life, perceiving suffering as an intellectual pleasure, and thought as superior to splendid folly. I suppose you made the wrong choice.

I can imagine you conversing with the existence you lost and keep missing so much, with the child you were long ago and perhaps still lives deep inside you.

Meanwhile you, in the midst of your inner fight, are searching for an ounce of the true you, struggling to break off the shackles, which, paradoxically, you love so strongly, because they wrap you not only with tormenting thoughts, but also with powerful defenses.

How strange it all sounds! The moment when we communicate with our Innermost Essence so horrifies us, that we cannot tell whether it was a blissful self-acceptance and reconciliation, or, rather, a blatant manifestation of narcissism.

Well, what expresses our self-love stronger than our self-hate? Narcissism reflects the most innocently charming part of us, that self-preoccupation and self-glorification, that hate of our innermost soul! isn't this paradox the ultimate purpose of existence?

It's exciting to hate oneself to the point of sublime love. It is like denying our obvious self-hate, and, unconsciously contradicting the cosmic laws, pretends to love ourselves above anything in the world. So how come our ultimate lover is incessantly haunted by all that melancholy and guilt?

The self-hater is actually a self-lover, who cannot tell love from hate, deeming them the same. After all, you cannot be preoccupied so much with what is not an object of adoration. You, too, my friend, is enamored with your inability to be what you perceive to be a normal human being. Yet you perceive those around you as normal just because you are not acquainted with their true minds. However, your envy of them grows constantly stronger. At the same time, you build up mental walls defending your detached observer's identity, which cannot and will not allow you to be like all the rest. Your essence and you are two separate entities who so bitterly rival each other and yet in love with each other to their very core; both of you take numerous guises, are visible and invisible to each other, and are engaged in endless deep conversations with and consult each other in many critical decisions.

Take off your guise!

How?

Unearth yourself!

Silence...

Be yourself!

Don't make me laugh! You know it's practically impossible in this alienated and masked world!

You must, you have to, your soul's essence will be destroyed unless you will become yourself at last! You have no choice!

You speak in marvelous theories, so give me a recipe, a design for conduct, a manner of perception...can you at least offer me some reasonable lie?

Well, you are, indeed, an outspoken existentialist, so bring out your existence, fire it up, experience it, enflame it with your life and burn in your own flame!

Now I close my eyes, examining my words through my emotions, which drag me into my inner fight. Now I wonder whether I have ever really wanted to become like "them", or maybe just be myself! Anyway, could have I ever be any different?

One cannot be anything beyond one's existing endless variety. Since one's world has been detached from whatever outside occurrence so far, it is as miraculously unique, as unprecedented as your plethora of emotions whenever you fall in love anew, since no love can ever resemble any previous one. Your torments, and your perception, probably taught you that only you could deal with your dark sides, and only your dark sides, but never with those of others, despite all your marvelous uniqueness. Neither could others, with your dark sides. So what can such an oldie like me do except embracing your oh-so-charming and oh-so-stinging thoughts?

Your phrase, that "no love can ever resemble any previous one", makes me smile, and will change my self-perception forever. From now onwards, I will never wish to be anything but myself, and probably love myself stronger than ever. Even if Happiness frequents me less than it does those around me, I will certainly draw comfort from the few magic moments of happiness that bless me, the person I will always appreciate!

Have you already manage to free yourself from that obsession to become what you are not?

Chapter Nine:
ON FREE WILL

◆ ◆ ◆

Since their tender age, some individuals have been instructed to fear an omnipresent and omniscient God. How hard it must feel, as a child, to think you are never left alone, never to live as free as your childish nature drives you! Then, suddenly, in a moment of enlightenment, the child asked the parents how he or she could make any choices, given that God already knows what one's choices would be? Upon hearing this question, they just went speechless, and then gave a crooked religious explanation, as if forced to reveal a dark secret, that "God knows the end of your road, yet it's up to you to take the turns". In other words, "Everything is foreseen; yet free will is given". To this, the child said nothing, supposedly believing them, since it was beyond him or her to contradict their words.

Hearing other children repeating the same story told by their parents, the child adheres to this conviction even stronger, which encircles him or her like a wall. Yet this wall is bound to crack someday, when one happens to meet children who heard other stories at home. I guess their conversation sounds like the following one:

It's not fair if He knows everything we will do in advance, since it means we can do nothing of our own!

Says who?! I do whatever I want all the time, without anybody knowing anything about it!

Says my mom and dad, who never lie to me!

My mom and dad never lie to me, either, and they told me no such stories!

Maybe because they don't have such an all-knowing God as we have!

We need no gods whatsoever; we can just play happily, as kids should!

Then, over supper, when asked about how one's day in school was, that child would explode with emotions reporting the event. Quite naturally, the parents would try to drive it home to their child these were ill-bred, bad children, to be kept away from, yet the child wouldn't understand how can children be bad.

However, even if these ideas are beyond one's understanding, nevertheless - probably out of filial piety – that child will only keep company to the right kids, found in the proper educational institutions.

It has always puzzled me why parents have to make up stories for their children about an omniscient God. I guess they adopted this concept because their parental love wasn't strong enough, so the all-seeing, caring God served them as an additional parental figure to watch over their child for them.

Bear in mind, my friend, that the parents, too, are victims of the same education, and know no other.

If all are brought up exactly as their parents were, where is free will? If the only worldview we deem right is what we hear at home, how can one take a new, ingenuous look at things, considering this will be as good as accusing one's parents of concealing the truth?

the scope of our free will seems to be very limited until a certain age, since until then, one undergoes an aggressive socialization process, and can be nothing but what society turns one into.

I find much more terrible the fact that it is always the most sublime and critical mental processes that take place early in life, as if humanity has mastered the art of mind-controlling since antiquity.

But how can parents bring up their beloved little ones except their own way?

Why must we assume there is just one right way at all? Why should your accidental place of birth define your faith, views and convictions, which make up the most essential parts of your mind? Isn't this a horribly dispiriting premise? It seems I have just expressed an idea most hard to accept: even if, when already grown up, the child may decide to discard the parent's beliefs, I doubt whether he or she could muster the courage it involves, taking a new road, without being haunted by that terrible guilt for discarding the parents' truth. We, who speak for the suppressed genuine souls, and who are familiar *with the powers of both love and guilt, must acknowledge that it would take an*

uncommon hero to take a new course towards re-generation, once true feelings

strive to manifest themselves.

Your questions triggered many speculations. For example, suppose the Pope was borne elsewhere, let's say, in India. In such a case, he would have been inspired with ideas and assumed titles completely different from the ones he professes and holds now - only because he was born and raised elsewhere. I am far from adhering to any "unquestionable" ideas or even strong beliefs, since my mind loves doubting. Yet those people are diametrically opposed to me, sticking to old acquaintances of the mind, indulging in them for the rest of their lives, never questioning their intellectual environment. The few who did muster the courage it takes to make their own choices, are haunted by hard feelings day and night, sometimes tormented by doubts whether trading the love and safety of their old world for all that solitude was worth it at all. Yet they must never focus on the moments of hardships, but examine their lives from a long-term perspective, over many years. Only then will they come to realize they lived a life that was true, experiencing their world as they really wanted to, in the bottom of their hearts. This is the greatest satisfaction a whole person could aspire to!

In this dialogue, we've just peeled off another layer of our mind, on our quest

for the deepest and truest core of human spirit, which only few dare explore.

Let me throw an even greater challenge at you, asking, "how come those choose not to make their choice?"

What did you have in mind? How can one choose not to make a choice?

Well, one may observe the response of a fellow who, when asked what he or she wishes for, says "I don't know", not due to ignorance, but due to inability to guess whether one's desire is in accordance with that of others. Therefore, that fellow fancies that the avoidance of decision is some convenient cavern to retreat to, in order to escape responsibility. However, neither what happens nor how society interprets one's conduct complies with one's expectations, since its others who decide for him or her, time and again. Thus, in the course of life, if a person prefers to obey

others, instead of making one's own choices, one may do it under the false religious excuse of modesty, presenting one's lifelong avoidance of making choices as a praiseworthy virtue.

So to what extent did you let others make your choices for you in the essential questions of your heart and mind?

Chapter Ten:
DISSOLVING IN "THEM"

◆ ◆ ◆

Among the numerous hardships every human must face is the necessity to deal with the views of others. On certain occasions, one needs the approval of one's circle desperately enough to resign one's free will to them, daring not to speak up one's mind, to the extent of voluntary dissolution in society, for the sake of feeling "belongingness".

Yes, it is hard to walk tall in human society.

Even those speaking out their mind boldly, might renounce it later on, just to avoid facing the solitude ultimate sincerity breeds, which is so terribly frightening.

I believe the sense of security which society offers the individual to be false and short-lived, since after a while the individual tries to restore one's true self and reason, until the next time one must face the multitude. Then, it's still the same old story of self-dissolving in the mob.

On the face of it, what you describe sounds like a win-win situation: the individual gains satisfaction from others' approval of one's social virtues, such as one's exemplary selflessness and other praises on the part of the rulers to one's self-degradation. On the other hand, once the individual recalls having his or her unique views and ambitions, which perhaps it is about time to speak out, the individual realizes right away he or she never

knew how to stand up to society, so one immediately resumes one's supposedly safe refuge, deep under the shade of others.

© Misha Gordin: The New Crowd

Moreover, others will inevitably fill the void left by the individual. That is to say, that if an individual resigns one's control of one's life, one consciously accepts the control of others. Hence, it doesn't matter whether one expressed one's submission explicitly, silently, or with some praises which sound self-degrading to the critical listener, since at any rate, it glorifies one's delicate, inward-oriented spirit. Thus, an individual unconfident of one's true colors, gets addicted to submission.

You and I are playing in mind – surgery. However, what about that poor fellow? Is it too late for that individual to reassume responsibility for one's life?

Your inner world illustrated to me the boundless nature of human spirit, which can re-generate itself at any age, by embarking on new courses, despite all the experiences and habits imprinted upon one's mind, which one cannot shake off.

Looking inside the head of an individual, whose mind is refined enough to discover one's responsibility for one's existence, we could see that person has reached the ultimate solitude, and is at a crossroad where one is the only decision maker. Naturally, that individual fears the Unknown, since it is the first time one must make one's own choices. But, see how one is empowered and invigorated once the road is taken, as if born again to live one's life anew - this time, to the full!

Even if one makes the wrong choice, one probably takes pride of one's courage, since it's oneself, not others who made the choice. Therefore, one should at least take pride for the courage of manifesting true selfness!

to what extent are you the captain of your own ship of life?

Chapter Eleven:
AN OUNCE OF HAPPINESS

◆ ◆ ◆

On certain mornings, I start off to a nearby park, equipped with a steaming cup of mint tea. Once I seat myself on a bench and let the sun caress me, my thoughts start running wild, reviving a magic childhood moment, of dashing aimlessly and smiling senselessly, overjoyed at the wind blowing at my face and all over me. We still have these moments, especially early in life, before we master the art of analyzing and comparing everything to everything else, and ourselves to others, and are just enchanted with almost everything around us. It is at those moments that we experience the purest joy imaginable. From there, I am carried away to another magic moment, of me devouring an entire chocolate cookie, all alone!

I am truly amazed at how infants dare to grasp their joy so explicitly, so blatantly, enjoying their life to the extent of insolence – demonstrating to us, grownups, we could be like them no more. Recalling my childhood, I see my happiness back then stemmed from habits I still love today, and I proud myself for that. I'm proud for preserving my pristine childish happiness in certain fields of life. Even though I realize that it gave me much greater happiness as a child, it doesn't make it any less pleasurable.

Moreover, the more distant memory my childhood turns into, the more I realize how hard it is to get even close to those heights of pure, pristine happiness. After all, in the grownups world, the way to happiness is a secret known to very few.

As a grown up, I came to recognize those forces constantly resisting my happiness - some of which emerged from deep within me. It's due to them that we sometimes fail to appreciate what we have, and even accept the most horrible realities as inevitabilities. Others always make us recall our happiest moment but paradoxically, they do not make us feel any better, but rather sadden us and make us feel lonely.

Quite a surprise, isn't it, to realize that in our very mind there are autonomous forces fighting us with such fierce defiance?

Cannot we purge this malady out of our minds?

Certainly not, since these are forces of nature, constantly at work, so our only choice is just to examine them with a mature, unconventional eye, in order to empower our present self.

Yet strangely, in spite of all my intellectual conclusions, I feel loneliness. So tell me, who are those impervious to it, those joy-coated ones who won their war on existential solitude?

Look, the greatest human minds have struggled with the horrible problem of existential solitude and expectation of blissful life. Honestly speaking, I advise you should seek no elixir of sincere and eternal happiness. All those best-selling guides for happiness are nothing but drugs addicting you to modern life's loneliness and insatiable misery.

How dare you discard that inherently human pursuit of the secret of happiness?

I came to realize, over the years, that contrary to what we read in fairy tales, human real life offers us no chance of constant happiness. I believe there never have been nor will ever be any constantly happy person. Coming to balance your magic moments, against your adverse moments, you will instantly see the latter ones outweigh the few fleeting moments of happiness. And I say it not as a grave pessimist, but because I wish to be true to myself.

In other words, despite one's momentary climaxes, it is difficult to experience the happiness we all pray for, isn't it?

Definitely, just a few of us capable of persistently adhering to existentialist philosophy which drives its followers to face the finiteness and ephemerality of humankind, as well as its associated solitude, and, as a result of these contemplations, fully appreciate the current state of things offers them.

However, despite dealing with such issues, which probably makes humans happier, one is still doomed to terrible travails and incessant setbacks while crusading for happiness. So where does our help come from?

It comes from one's mature insights, exclusively.

Look, my sincerity compels me to acknowledge that all my happiness so far only lasted for a few seconds at a time, here and there. At best, I never had more than a ten-minute long true Nirvana, when I experienced the Higher Existence. Everyone can imagine several moments in life of pure happiness, with no falsehood. Those-usually rich and famous - who are presumed happy, are actually not. In fact, most of them are in a state of abysmal depression, their presumed happiness being nothing but a façade.

The stronger my awareness of my moments of happiness has grown, and the more clearly I recognized the actions that drove me to ecstasy, the more frequently I tried to indulge in them. Moreover, I realized how wise it is to expand, constantly, the fields where you can generate your ounces of happiness. In our world of detachment and alienation, we all must specialize in generating our moments of happiness. Due to this growing awareness, I also discovered the value of spontaneity and serendipity.

In other words, what you actually ask me is not only to regard new experiences open-mindedly, but also to be mindful of my experiences proved to be - a sources of happiness and stimulators of self-fulfillment. It sounds innocent, in some mature way, since we are accustomed to grow bored by and alienated from old practices. Yet you not only look on them favorably, but even most appreciatively, almost like a child excited by one's elementary actions.

You've just made me smile. Being thrilled like children always feels great. Looking closer at the human pursuit of ultimate happiness, we may find out that its true objective is not our own happiness, but rather the belief in us being happier than others, or at least the others' belief in our happiness surpassing theirs. After all, hardly ever do we betray our unhappiness in public, concealing it with cunning we've mastered over the years. So let's stop deluding ourselves: those others conceal their true self just as cunningly, so where does it lead us all? Why must we always think our happiness must be at another's expense? Why can't we regard happiness as a win-win situation, rather than a 'zero-sum game'. Why do I feel lonely and miserable, while a fellow-human observing me might mistake me for the happiest of mortals? I acknowledge that the misery or happiness in the bottom of an individual's heart is undetectable by outside observers, who might misinterpret one's condition. Still, the actual source of our unhappiness is that we are all too weak to afford looking fragile. Why haven't we learned to accept reality? How can we quit that futile pursuit of ultimate happiness, settling, instead, for our ounce of wonderful, serendipitous and modest happiness, which requires not epic exploits and experiences, but rather homely and familiar ones? Why cannot we look for our happiness inwards, rather than outwards? These are questions yet to be addressed...

You spoke most sincerely, and from your words, I gather that it is a great virtue to acknowledge one's constant unhappiness which humanity so glorifies as every mortal's aspiration. Nevertheless, tell me, where else can I find comfort whenever I rise to another unhappy morning, except in my fantasy of happiness? On certain occasions, that fantasy seems like our only motive and energy to fight another day. To be completely honest, an individual - that includes even me - feels good about looking happier than others, since it infuses one with a sense of power and with many other wonderful feelings, which I believe those others to enjoy as much as oneself. This way we, the pseudo-happy ones shine for the rest of humanity, which is submerged in their misery. Then, when our wheel of fortune turns, it's others who seemingly never lose their smiles while we, the miserable masses, try to share their happiness. But, due to the tricks of our immature ego, their happiness fails to move us a bit. Well, we at least nobly and happily share their anguishes.

Dialogues like the present one make me believe that some would try to suppress this truth as long as they live. Therefore, I find it a rare privilege to discuss these issues openly, shedding our conventional suppression and timidity. After all, my time is short and my capacity of revealing the fascinating and complex mysteries of existence seems magical to me. Believe me, right now I am overwhelmed with joy for sharing with you my innermost emotions.

So who is the source of happiness in your Play of Life? What gives you your ounce of happiness?

Chapter Twelve:
ON GREAT HEARTS

◆ ◆ ◆

What better gift can one wish for, than a wholehearted smile intended for him or her?

Certainly, your smile is a window of your love.

Even if one's heart is coated with a thick armor of detachedness, one smile can breach through it all. What greater stratagem can be then an infant's enchanting smile?

Oh, that one is absolutely irresistible! It just impregnates any human's heart

easily!

Moreover, upon seeing an infant's smile, one is not only excited, but also presumes it to be the infant's first smile ever, addressed particularly at him.

So this smile reaches for fellow-human's heart.

One may wonder whether the infant's parents actually generated a great heart, rather than merely a child.

what a magnificent masterpiece a newborn is, so pure and free of existential

maladies! By masterpiece, I mean not one's perfect outward beauty, but one's pristine soul, with its unlimited capacity. Bearing child is like creating a completely new universe.

It seems that "great heart" of the newborn shrinks, little by little, over the years, worn off from everyday life.

By contrast, how proud are the parents for their children's accomplishments, as if their sole purpose in this world is just scoring high grades and winning diplomas, while letting their hearts grow numb?

I am very saddened to hear such observations. What is our struggle for life and death over socially valued prizes all about, if it costs humans their natural love and compassion? Isn't it much better to be great-spirited, rather than, say, a great psychiatrist?

If only parents knew they should cherish their dear little ones' great hearts like rare treasures, instead of just launching them into this world's rat race, totally unprepared, we would've needed therapists at all!

Certainly not! But what a surprise it is, to find you so great-hearted! Even your smile seems hearty all of a sudden.

Well, old folks like me, by the time they address existential questions, can afford shedding off all the facades and pretenses from which we suffered all our lives. Far from feeling grateful for the deception I was trained to practice, I yearn to its opposite, that is, my pristine, childish sincerity. It allowed me to fool around and let myself smile once again, feeling free from any social obligations, just as I was in my infancy.

Is this the reason for the wonderful daring of some elderlies to go dancing in public, all of a sudden, despite a lifelong timidity and introversion? Is

this what allows them to admit their major embarrassments, having to answer to no one nor caring about their public image any longer?

Certainly, because all of a sudden it strikes them that this may be their last chance of having certain experiences and sensations, nearly as intense as the ones they had when they had any first experience, as if their Play of Life tries to come full circle. The difference is that we, the old folks, as opposed to the young ones, already know how time flies, and, to be completely honest, I'm afraid we don't always realize just how fast it flies.

Exactly, younglings like me live as if tomorrow never comes, while in your circle, the flight of time is painfully evident, since those around you depart from this world much more frequently.

Keep away from these heavy thoughts, and just indulge in the happy innocence of an infant's smile, even if it is marked on my plain-looking face! See how it becomes me to go dancing in the street, as if there is nobody else in the world to notice me. Can't you see it?! Why should I wait all those decades to enjoy that? Just have mercy on yourself, and resign to your heart's desire! Instead of observing the world, go create your own worlds! Fall in love with the world, as if it is your own boundless playground! Or, as I put it - be a Great Heart which accepts no bounds!

Chapter Thirteen:
ON HUMAN KINDNESS

◆ ◆ ◆

Suppose you could ask a person just one question, to receive a definite answer, what would it be?

I would try to figure out what drives one to pursue justice in what sometimes seems like a chaotic world.

What about you? How would you answer your own question?

Instantly, I phrased the question more sympathetically: since one is addicted to pleasant feelings, the sense of justice affects him like a drug.

In such a world, one only has a sense of one's own peculiar justice, since others

might perceive justice differently.

So one persistently stands one's ground. What has justice got to do with it?!

Sadly, this is so. All one does seems to be for one's own good, while we—so we

believe, strive to sacrifice for our fellow-humans, don't we?

Well, we kind of pray, or, if you wish, hope it would be so. Let me sincerely confess to another sentiment: occasionally, I pass by a God-forsaken person, who seems to realize there is nobody in the entire universe who

misses or cares about him. When our eyes meet, I am overwhelmed with shame for not facing my fears of becoming like him some day. This drives me to look the other way, to ignore this possibility. What is worse, I have already realized that what drives us to charitable acts is not necessarily empathy or the wish to relieve others' miseries, but rather to wash away our own souls' miseries.

From here follows, that one's righteousness is nothing but an escape!

Being miserable through righteousness is definitely better than complete disregard!

Certainly!

So how come Good serves as the façade of this inevitability, which is Evil, and cannot exist in its own right, if this whole Play of Life must have some director?!

Beware of this question! Rephrase it, smooth up your mind, and present your world clearly to me!

Just look at an aloof stranger, examining the hue of his eyes and the wrinkles Fate marked in his face, and instantly, you'll see you can have at least a little glimpse into his soul. Yet you are still ignorant of his infinite uniqueness, and of all the countless evolutions his inner world has gone through. After all, even he himself is unaware of all the layers of his own mind, since it is only occasionally that our thoughts cross the threshold of our consciousness. My introspection has taught me that those who can access their higher consciousness are very few, since what's the use of knowing that sometimes, your kindness stems from your fear to face your fellow's misery?! What is praiseworthy about it?! Nonetheless, instead of wiping out their fellow-humans' misery, by eradicating poverty with a snap of a finger- as they could have done, humans love giving, mistaking it for Good which fills their hearts with pride. Can it be that the poor only exist for the givers, whose worst fear is that the poor may be gone away?

Did you mean: once the poor are gone, could the givers boost their pride so easily? I think that only now I understand you: nobody is innocently or selflessly good, since one only gives charity to glorify oneself or disregard a fellow-human's misery, under the excuse of pursuing Right and for indulging

in other self-praises. Is that the point you tried to make?

The very point! Yet do not presume me mournful, since not only have I learned to search into the abyss of human soul, but also recognize the magic manifestations of life, finding the innocent, disinterested Good in the magic of colorful flowers, and the endless expressions of art in living creatures. I even managed to love humanity, since I have experienced a true love".

Coming back to your first question, it makes one immediately wonder whether

a human cannot reach for the abstract Right, but only yearn for a tight

embrace confirming one's own existence. One may also wonder whether a

person's misgivings about the outside world only reflect one's inner world, as

if he had turned the world into a stage presenting nothing but his own mind,

even unconsciously".

Why should we care about these misgivings in our dialogues, where we can cut open and probe whatever we wish, like master surgeons, for whom nothing is beyond reach? What other explanation can any person find for one's need to understand fellow-humans, except the evident desire to understand, first and foremost, oneself? Yet while pondering on these problems of the mind, we refine ourselves, constantly learning about both the hidden as well as the visible aspects of ourselves - which are nothing but another layer through which we can probe to reach our secrets. It conceals the blatant truth like a masterfully designed mask".

What about that angel of solitude, in whose eyes you recognized this reality

down to its minutest details? How come he survives in this world, being so

lonely he had already forgotten the caressing touch of his mother's hand, and

even the memory of her look have grown vague in his mind? Look at him, how

he sits, all bent down, facing all the passers-by day by day, yet never gives up looking in the crowd for those who loved him and forsook him in other times. From another point of view, no less brutal and horrible one, maybe he found his purpose in life in relentlessly probing the conscience of people whose eyes incessantly meet his eyes, which swarm with stories. It is through this inner lifelong struggle that he unconsciously teaches his disregarders the meaning of deep solitude, since humans avoid loneliness like a plague. Yet he persistently throws at them his deepest emotions, thus softening their hearts like a wizard, without noticing it himself!

He lives completely in the dark, since the crowd's eyes have grown utterly blind to others' plight, as if compassion had been purged out their hearts until they grew numb. He who had fallen to the lowest abyss of pain knows no other way but striving desperately to resume one's intimate and compassionate look at his fellow-humans' souls, because he cannot handle that horror which reduces him to dust.

As a matter of fact, those whose hearts went numb to the fear of others degrade the forsaken one worse that the rough-hearted who dismiss his misery with a glance or quickly walk away. The latter at least deal with it in a way. Once, he saw a mother covering her son's eyes to keep him from seeing the misery, but a few steps later the child's eyes were drawn to that man, as if he was wondering, unconsciously, why the man lived there, of all places. Such scenes are as a mental embrace for him, since he most definitely knows that human hearts are essentially good, and only grow numb when facing the horror of life!

Well, we've already examined all that while searching for justice, but where does it dwell? After millennia of searching, horror still engulfs humankind like air. Maybe we will eventually find out that it's the pursuit of justice, rather than justice itself that sublimes us, since the realization

of Right, as opposed to what we've learned until now, is not what is important?

This play, called Pursuit of Justice will never stop, since fear will never cease, forever assuming various guises. Therefore, humans must always struggle with it, since without that struggle, they would lack any drive for sublimation and advancement, but rather give up dreaming, indulging in satisfaction!

As far as I see it, a human's strife for Justice is nothing but an attempt to be great-hearted until one's very end, to keep the Play of Life from subjugating one's heart to darkness, the world, from shrinking our soul to its bounds, and oneself, sensing others souls.

So how numb has your own heart grown so far, since your infancy?

Chapter Fourteen:
THE AGONY OF THINKING

◆ ◆ ◆

My elementary school's class teacher once praised me-sarcastically, I guess - for "asking good questions". Upon Hearing that, I wondered how these questions came into being in the first place, since I made no special efforts to conceive them. Sometimes I regarded my questions as mere outbursts of insolence, sophisticatedly disguised as curiosity. It is only now, many years later, that I came to appreciate my questions as attempts of doubting everything.

Shouldn't every educator aspire to bring up generations of critical minds, who never stop doubting and questioning? What is question else than a manifestation of mental progress? How easy it is to settle for bringing up a generation of mindless conformists, identical to one another except in appearance? Yet ironically, it was in that convention-factory called "elementary school", that this class teacher encountered me - the unusual exceptional student, who managed to intrigue him with questions trespassing the conventional bounds of discussion, compelling him, too, to overcome one's inherent limitations. All of a sudden, I stopped feeling shame and started taking pride in my original questions-at least deep inside me, as if they confirmed my individuality.

We have already addressed, in our previous dialogues, the problem of societies "knowledge factories", which are only designed to spread the received wisdom and conventional values of specific times and places. Only exceptional individuals manage to traverse the bounds of convention imprinted on them in a years-long process. Yet the true thinker and doubter can do no other. Such a person cannot grow to become just another conformist, trading one's responsible way of life for the blissful ignorance of the mob — if one does, the mob will dictate their values, views and perspectives on life for him or her. Look at you: how, as a youth, you always questioned everything, attempting to create your own world using your own intellect, instead of resigning your identity completely.

Nevertheless, sometimes I feel as if doubting and questioning infuse the individual not with confidence and self-esteem, but, on the contrary, with terrible sense of insecurity and impotence, compared to all those intellectually cloned, who live most proudly and confidently. How can they?

It depends not on capacity, but on audacity. Since asking existential questions involves great anguish, individuals tackling them are very uncommon. Instead of dealing with these questions, humankind prefers to suppress them masterfully. As a result, those who do dare to tackle them, tend to withdraw to themselves - from where they can examine their world with awe. This highly courageous act is appreciable.

Somehow, I feel as if all original thoughts are stored in some magical cloud high above, which lets, most sparingly, an occasional drop to water a human mind. Yet this single drop is full of so much wisdom, that it germinates in that mind a wonderful enlightenment translated into action. It is time to declare openly that humans scarcely have any thoughts of their own, yet they are terribly proud for the few ones they do have, as if they have created their own world with their infinite wisdom. I, unlike them, in some magic moments, imagine I fly high above this wonderful planet, looking down at it, amazed at my smallness and the modest role I play in it. Yet paradoxically, it is these moments that make

me fully experience my existence, making me feel as if I create my own world. Since it's I who present all these challenging existential questions, they reinvigorate me, making me view my life like an infant observing an insect, considering its existence utterly insignificant. Likewise, I, observing the rest of the universe, doom it to absolute insignificance. My persistent questions nearly destroyed the world I created for myself, one of them nearly compelling me to cave in. Yet the courageous, undeterred minds constantly destroy and regenerate themselves.

It is most wonderful, my friend! Therefore, fear not your doubts and questions, even if they, instead of bringing you peace of mind, only breed more doubts expanding into a bottomless pit, where, paradoxically, you are driven despite all the anguish and travails it has in store for you. Nevertheless, you have the courage it takes to plunge into the abyss of seemingly crippling authenticity, suffering self-inflicted injuries, only to recover and keep fighting this forlorn-hope battle, consciously, just because you can do no other.

I believe that endless immersion in the abyss of doubting is just a self-deception for the sake of self-glorification, an unconscious way of fancying yourself as the Savior of Mankind who will magically bestow peace of mind on fellow-combatants. Yet, despite one's awareness of the futility of that fight, one cannot shake off that sublime delusion.

Well, we must realize that the key to answering the great questions, which preoccupy humanity since the dawn of history, is individuals' truth to themselves and their self-consciousness, but most importantly, humans' recognition of their inability capacity of learning.

What about you? Have you ever had any questions you suppressed just for your fear of society's response?

Chapter Fifteen:
MY FAREWELL PARTY.

◆ ◆ ◆

Look, I tried to avoid this subject, but I guess I can't help it. In the twilight of my life, I am haunted by thoughts about my Farewell Party.

What party did you have in mind?

I mean that moment when all my dear ones escort me to the Great Beyond, to the green fields watered with tears of love and yearning, when they lavish me with all the praises I had never been lucky enough to hear. I'm sure you got the idea already.

As reluctant as I might be to think about it, I see what is on your mind. So please tell me how you envision that party.

Well, it feels somewhat awkward to describe what I, most probably, will never experience, does't it? However, I definitely know what I wish not to see on my last farewell.

Please, elaborate.

I wouldn't like it to drive my dear ones to any mourning, anguish, or horror, but inspire them with the opposite sentiments.

Is it possible?! Outburst of crying is the most natural and inevitable response of a mournful person.

Well, I wish them to shed for me tears of joy, for all the pleasures life offered me, rather than deplore their loss at my departure.

Nonetheless, I will definitely cry missing you, since you were my magic mentor.

It takes a great courage to cry, which sometimes I failed to muster or recognize the immensity of understanding it indicates. Yet now, my introspection taught me the art of crying joyfully and resigning to excitement shamelessly. However, my friend, what I intended was to tell you about some wonderful farewell Party I had attended several years ago...

Tell me more!

We parted then from Rafael, an old friend, an unstoppable joker, who always kept smiling. His wonderful mind always managed to perceive the brightest sides of life, despite the all-too-real calamities he had lived through: his parents had been struggling for many years with dementia, and one day, on a regular medical check-up, he was diagnosed with pancreatic cancer. The doctors gave him just a few weeks to live. Passionately in love with his life, he was resolved not to let reality dispirit him. Therefore, he carefully planned his own funeral, which thrilled us in a most wonderful way. His coffin stood open in his parish church, where all his dear ones paid him their last respect. Two of them were half laughing, half crying. When I approached, to kiss him for the very last time, I couldn't believe just how masterfully he mocked at his fate: his yellowish skin was covered with a T-shirt decorated with the similarly yellow face of Homer Simpson. The perfect composition of their colors was enough to make me smile. But here's the best of it: under Homer's face, which made all of us laugh for so many years, I detected the hilarious sentence concluding Monty Python's comedy Life of Brian:

"Always look on the bright side of life"

I instantly betrayed a melancholic smile, my mind - overwhelmed with a blend of horror and happiness - brightly enlightened at this dark moment: the very feelings Rafael wanted us to experience that day. This taught me to look at life from the right perspective, of acceptance and contentment.

Was that a surprising confession! I never imagined people could give such Farewell Parties, which give their participants so much joy!

Bear in mind life always offers you joys, even at Ultimate Farewell Parties!

It makes perfect sense. So, how did you envision your own funeral?

Curiously, when asked to describe their own funeral, people are stricken with genuine existential horror, since it compels them to retell their life-stories from their loved ones' perspectives. Once they elaborate on it, they come to reveal their innermost and sincerest wishes - for the very first time in life! Yet I, who am already aware of that, can envision my very last farewell, which I am to conduct from high above, in some super-logical manner. I guess I would like it to be a cheerful, inspiring event, preferably with some gifted comedian telling humorous anecdotes about me, making people cry over me for the right reasons. I would like to conclude it with an orchestra playing Vivaldi's Four Seasons and some celebrity folk singer performing Oldies but Goldies. This will make me happy even after death.

I would like to wish you this event will never takes place, yet at the same, I know it will, so I'll be happy to enjoy your party.

I highly appreciate that. Let me tell you it is most impressive to be willing to resign to death so calmly, thus somewhat immortalizing our current friendship. The point is, he who is willing to part this world proudly, keeps one's spirit alive until one's very last moment, through constant self-destruction and self-regeneration. Many times, I reached such high levels of consciousness, and experienced moments of such powerful joy, which allowed me to accept my demise with complete resignation. It was because deep down, I could see my life from the right perspective, thus enhancing momentary pleasures, making the most of them, like our Inner Child who cries "Gosh, what a great day!" Such a person is constantly inspired with such emotions, making one think he or she achieved the climax of joy life can offer!

Well, I'm amazed at the way you managed to bring your carefree Inner Child into this rather heavy dialogue.

It's elementary: what except innocent, childish, lively perspective could drive one to conceive such a masterful manipulation of our minds like that of my dear Rafael?

So how do you envision your farewell party?
Will it enhance your resolution to realize,
right now, your latent desires?

Chapter Sixteen:
THE PRESENT ANGUISH

◆ ◆ ◆

Where can the greatest pain hit a human?

In our hearts, so they say.

Our hearts?

Indeed, our hearts and minds.

And what is on a human's mind throughout one's life?

Events of unreal times.

Correct, but what are those times?

Our past and future.

What about our present?

Even though it is real, the anguish and fears it generates are nowhere near those born out of past facts and future prospects.

However, even the great present anguish can crudely produce some insights on our past and future.

Such as...?

Such as the immediate response to the loss of a beloved person, which is feeling guilt for past events, and doubting one's very existence in the near future.

But why, paradoxically, our greatest anguish is generated by non-present events?

This is a great puzzlement. I have been seriously enquiring into it.

Can this very examination of unreal times serve as an escape from the terrible present plights of our mind?

This is an intriguing theory, since there is no reason why we should instantly succumb to these crippling thoughts.

Therefore, contrary to what I assumed before, perhaps the greatest of human pains result from our present. However, their reluctance to face their "here and now" honestly, drives humans to pry into their psyche, eventually coming up with neurotic ideas about fanciful worlds - just to escape their present menace. This can account for several human behaviors.

What else can we deduce from it?

For instance, that human psyche is so complex, as to drive an individual to disregard, willingly, one's present throughout most of one's adult lifetime, making him preoccupied with those fanciful Other Worlds and those unreal times, namely past and future.

In that case, if everybody is preoccupied with the events of unreal times, who are those who actually live "here and now"?

Those who to this must be full of magical meditative stratagems.

What about you? Can you entirely detach yourself from this world, at least for a few minutes, in order to experience a moment of complete sincerity, rather than being haunted by guilt for your past and fears from your future?

Chapter Seventeen:
THE TRICKS PSYCHE PLAYS ON US

◆ ◆ ◆

I have witnessed many inexplicable phenomena, yet none was as inexplicable as the attempts of some individuals to fend off healthy joy as if it was some deadly plague, with loathing-twisted lips, resistant to spontaneous kindness. They inadvertently chose to be bitter at life, obsessed with petty complaints about the irresistible Evil and unwilling to see any bright blossom. Those terrible individuals, whose company is practically unbearable, will never accept the joy of others, dismissing it with miserly smiles, as if fearing to run out of their reserve of happiness. They are incapable of enjoying any success, compliment, or admirer's embrace, since they deem themselves as undeserving any of those. Those lovers of mental torments embrace the sufferer's character in order to avoid experiencing the metamorphoses life brings about, or maybe even life itself. What a waste it is to look at your unrepeatable life from such a bilious perspective, always as an outside observer, experiencing nothing!

There are always such characters around us, as if, by some law of nature, every company must have its self-proclaimed propagator of alienation and suffering, detaching oneself from any human company or experience. The only raison d'etre of such a person is to play the sufferer in that company. It's beyond me to figure out what draws them to the darkest, repelling abyss of the soul, rather than to happy smiles, which, as fake as they might be, still stimulate the momentary secretion of happiness hormone.

We are already aware of the outward, socially unacceptable effects of depression, since open and public expressions of fear and sincere feelings became as undesirable as some infectious microbes, which must be isolated as soon as possible. Nonetheless, society still capable of some honest recognition of the experience of the depressed, who seem to be the ones telling the whole truth to society's face, while most of us conceal our truth behind fake smiles. Those people manifest the honesty of Biblical Prophets, whose words were too truthfully painful for anybody to heed.

You seem to have taken the diametrically opposed stand, making me see things differently all of a sudden. Those whose conduct or even perspective we can hardly accommodate are nothing but aspects of ourselves, the expression of which we violently suppress, yet we never doubt their sincerely expressed truths. Am I right?

Absolutely! Every human has a dark side, which can easily emerge in one's everyday perceptions. One may take the course of pseudo-realistic survival strategy of making enormous mental efforts in order to find the bright sides of any darkness, like some legendary explorer's trick, a wonderful magic or a sci-fi author's ploy. this is the very way to save yourself from the effects of sincerely expressed truth of the depressed, without coming to deny the reality of the outside world or the consequences of one's actions at all. From a religious point of view, we may describe this as acting above reason, on a higher level of perception. Just remember all the great creators who lived a life of suffering.

This is anything but easy. In order to maintain an optimistic perspective of a world that must otherwise seem dismal to any normal eye, one must live in an imaginary world.

Given that people all around us suffer great anguish, all the time, and our loved ones might depart this world at any moment, our mind's last resort seems to be just mourning our existence. Yet ironically, it is these very moments of existential horror that tell us we have two choices: either keep struggling with a real, endless anguish, while going on living our unrepeatable lives, or succumb to that endless anguish, thus, unintentionally, surrendering one's vitality. After all, as some wonderful old tune taught us, "dreams are our reality". Paradoxically, perhaps it is our unconscious choice to live in order to meet our inevitable end, that surrenders us to that endless, debilitating anguish.

It's all too easy to focus on our inevitable end. But look at all the travails we have to face in our everyday life, which are just as challenging. These, too, reveal the great spirits - in both young and old bodies - capable of resurrecting from numerous downfalls, recognizing the inevitability of anguish in our lives, yet fighting on proudly and smilingly.

Introspection, too, can inspire us with a bright perspective, commonly known as optimism. Wisely examining your past, you can decide not to let events get under your skin, denouncing their ill effects and hypnotizing yourself into creating a wonderful new you. That new you lives through the very same experiences you do, yet is focused on that pure bright ounce of it, living it to the full over and over, as if nothing else exists.

What a nice survival tactic is obliviousness, what a gift it is for humankind! However, it might drive us to deny our very reality: even if others keep remembering events we have already forgotten, including those we witnessed, we conveniently erase them from our own minds. In order to save myself from experiencing the horror once again, I just decide that some truths are not worth knowing.

By contrast, if you are true to yourself, you recognize the reality of anguish, but also master the art of tricking your mind into creating moments counterbalancing those of anguish, thus achieving stability and tranquility. The capacity of fracturing your life's experience, combined with the gift of obliviousness, allows you to experience life selectively, thus living, an optimistic, powerful and gratifying life.

Well, it seems that both pessimists and optimists can benefit from their worldviews. The former ones experience the truth, as bleak as it may seem, while the latter ones always manage to out-trick their mind magically, and both of them manage to keep on living and adhere to their states of mind forged by their choices. Yet eventually, both go through the same arduous course in life, more or less, so making yourself smile your life away seems wiser than just wallowing in your anguish, no matter how true it is. If our course of life only consists of rugged trails, with no roadmaps, in a world where darkness prevails, the only strategy of survival is through smiling, but only after a thorough understanding of our blind Fate, which devours us all, even the best of us - including you, dear friend.

You managed to capture this deep idea perfectly, in a brief yet profound way. So always bear in mind that whenever you manage to negotiate an obstacle through seeing it from the miraculously and enchantingly correct perspective, you generate a brave new inner you, free of anguish, which can only slightly emerge on your outside, while you tightly cling to the wonderful aspects of your life as if they are the only reality.

From here clearly follows that despite humankind's inclination to bleakness, the courageous mind can set you on a different, exciting course. Naturally, it takes years of mental preparations, which is hardly what Everyman wishes to undertake!

For your general knowledge, even the bleak perspective on life has its advantages. That is to say, it helps you deepen those crypts which enhance your identity, and which you are well aware of, no matter how hard you try to conceal them. This way you can create a peculiar identity fed by the repulsion and depression, or even the unwilling fascination you generate in those around you. Such perspective can make a certain behavior which otherwise might seem erratic, look reasonable. Since such a person's psyche is a world of simmering fears, keeping him from intimacy, one feels safer never to touch them in order to avoid getting burnt. This concealment can last an entire lifetime, and is entirely senselessly. after all, even a painful burn can be exciting, since it makes you feel, while the choice to fear a feeling might disable you from sincere intimate acquaintance not only with fellow-humans, but even with yourself. While it is not easy to learn to love oneself, and the capacity of loving the reality around you, no matter how painful, is a privilege of the highest souls. Contrary to what the commoners are taught, loving reality means more than just gratefulness for everything that happens to you. It involves magnificently sophisticated stratagems manipulations of the mind.

I, due to years of observation, have learned to detect the effects of your inner struggle in your eyes. Others, however, despite their lifelong experience, may remain practically blind to how those around them delve into their own existential abyss and useless complaints against it, which can generate nothing but silent despair or abhorrence of one's present. You're supposedly blind to the horrors of reality, yet you are far from being innocent. To the contrary, you have that bold sophistication which unsettles everyone attentively observing your responses to the world. It allows you to make these responses with such a natural nonchalance. While those around you may be infuriated at your perspective, they are at the same time amazed at your tranquility. This, in turn, prevents you from succumbing to self-tormenting – Known as the most widespread human trait. You, most defiantly, refuse to share this trait, outright dismissing any doubts of whether this reluctance is of any use or whether it will make you look as a man of no empathy. There is an ocean of empathy in you, yet you are too sincere to let your fellow-human's inner struggle overwhelm you with that fellow's sorrow. You, always willing to share the pain of others, will be there for them, and do much more than that: once the storm subsides and the tears dry out, you will know how to see the bright sides of life, which makes life worth living, thus practically reanimate your fellow-humans.

Look well into the choices you make: is your glass always half-empty, or half full?

Chapter Eighteen:
SUCH LOVE

◆ ◆ ◆

Love is the stuff poetry and the arts are made of. It thrills and affects us all, who presume to experience true love. But do we really know anything about love? Have you, dear friend, ever loved?

You have this strange habit of amazing me with a straightforward question, changing the subject right afterwards! First, let me properly absorb the first part of your phrase, which I object outright! How dare you doubt that all humans , since time immemorial, experienced love?!

What is it that you object so outright?

Don't you acknowledge that humans may either experience a brief infatuation or long love affairs, or even fall in love again with each other - at least once in a while?

As for what poets say, don't you think they portray human emotions rather truthfully? Do you really believe all love literature to be groundless fantasy, having nothing to do with normal human hearts? How could have all these authors moved your heart, unless they believed they could accurately target your mind?

Start thinking out of the box of human conscious will. Soar up and away, to your higher consciousness, reaching for your deeper self. Once you notice all the numerous manifestations of love, you'll see, for a moment, the difference between a love one chooses out of sincere intimacy, as opposed to a love one picks up accidentally, like a stranger's compliment to indulged in. Look at all human attachments driven by benefits, which have nothing to do with love.

How terrible it feels to recognize that this truth was always deep inside me, despite all my attempts to hide from it. I must admit there is a gulf between the loves of my adolescence and the flame of love consuming me currently, as if I have never loved before. It makes me feel ashamed and awkward, and I guess many feel just the same, yet prefer the self-congratulatory delusion.

Well, we are all under this delusion, occasionally. Can you imagine a life with nothing like the fire of your current love? Haven't you just expressed the strongest regret any human could ever have!?

How could a person grow accustomed to succumbing to that horrendously wonderful madness of love, which consumes one from within and drive him or her to willingly lose any control of one's life - for the sake of some pleasure, only to be left with a void in life after a while?

What a hard blow of absolute sincerity!

Not a hard blow, but the way to wonderful mindfulness! Since life often grows more complicated than you wish it to, even a bright-burning love can die out, for a variety of mundane reasons. It attests to your vitality, rather than to your failure.

Vitality? Come on! We're talking about a broken heart and goddamn incessant melancholy, especially when you lack the courage it takes to take a new course in life unless driven by a disaster, aren't we?

Melancholy is a natural and proper response, just like in case of mourning, but it also indicates regeneration, since this is your most sublime existence. You must never betray your true self for the devil you know, since you can ascent to these heights, time and again! Accept it as a given that a human heart can contain countless loves, without any of those loves diminished a bit: the love of one's children, life partner, family, friends, and obviously, of oneself!

Your words are most optimistic and empowering, since one who had already loved so intensely might believe that such love is unrepeatable, despite one's currant anguish. Yet, at a closer look at one's soul, you could see clearly that one still loves most intensely in all aspects of life. Once you believe in yourself, realizing that your life constantly transforms, you can turn over a new page, indulging in a passion as innocent and more intense than you ever had! This is the greatest miracle.

You spoke most accurately. A Human heart knows no bounds, and all attempts to subjugate it to reason are doomed to fail: for example, I can love two individuals at the same time, and can't help it, even though it is socially unacceptable.

How can you have two objects of love at the same time? Doesn't it feel like an emotional burden?

It is no burden at all, since a human heart is naturally inclined to love and give as much as possible, and it feels most natural, as if I have known no other - as indeed I haven't! Yet I was exposed, by complete surprise, to the flame consuming my soul. it is that miraculous palpitation and felicitous expansion of my heart that demonstrate to me the human capacity of trespassing the bounds of social norms and received wisdom.

Bear in mind that only a few can accept "sharing" their beloved ones with others. Don't you consider it a terrible injury to your first love?

Wouldn't I have terribly injured myself if I didn't love with all my might, that is, if I wasn't who I truly am?

I am no longer certain of anything, feeling increasingly insecure and vulnerable.

This also was my immediate and quite natural response to my failed romance, but as you and I realize, I can only live my own life, so I cling to it passionately, making decisions which sometimes are incompatible with the feelings of others, since I just cannot denounce such a significant part of me, come what may.

Applying your philosophy to my own life, I see that my current needs and conditions are not the same as those of my youth, since times are changing and driving people to new and wonderful realms, which we had no idea about earlier in life. So what will they do now? Will they confine themselves or discover unknown aspects of their souls, letting themselves follow their heart's desires? Once again, our inner true self, with all its suppressed fantasies, explodes at our faces. Therefore I, too, no matter how hard it seems, must look into my hidden thoughts, asking myself whether I have any suppressed fantasies I would have followed if I had the courage it takes.

It is not about courage or suppression, but about positive and negative reinforcements. In other words, look at the sublime humans who taught humanity how to love their fellow-humans as themselves. We all consider this a marvelous achievement, and welcome such people with admiring smiles whenever we sense their presence near us. Yet these very people always tried to

EXISTENTIAL DIALOGUES | 83

tell you how and under what restrictions and reservations to love your fellow-humans - can there be a greater hypocrisy?

One who loves can only do it his or her unique way, with no need of any instructions or restrictions. Humans have an innate capacity for love, so they need no love counseling. To be honest, once two bodies and souls unite, they can do no other than love madly, even without the arousing touch.

To conclude your words: love, that magic interpersonal communication, has no rules, and whenever such rules were made, they proved useless. As the Bible puts it, "the more they were oppressed, the more they multiplied and the more they spread abroad" (Ex. 1:12).

So when was the last time your heart was overflowing with passion?

Chapter Nineteen:
DREAMS

♦ ♦ ♦

I feel a dream building up inside me, about me, engulfing and sort of manipulating me, even though it is predominated by horror. Yet that horror excites and inspires me. It allows me to observe myself from above, while I walk alongside my loved one who is smiling at me. I am overwhelmed with satisfaction that only looks, not words can express. An alien surprised us, assaulting my beloved, which makes even the heart of a calm person like me terrified lest he might hurt her. My heart runs wild, driving me to yell at him to let her go, and then, force him to the ground, while she, terrified like hell, flees away from that evil.

It attests to how strongly you love her, doesn't it? Or, maybe something completely different was on mind then?

What was on my mind was why we dream so much about our own courage.

What else should humans dream of, their miserable helplessness?

Dreams appear to serve as a borderline between a terrible abyss and the wonderful, which are two dichotomous realms. What makes you wake up from a dream is either an ecstasy or a horrible shame for a failure. Most of my dreams started with horror yet ended with blissful tranquility, like a heart-stirring music falling silent surprisingly.

A dream with a horrible conclusion might reveal your innermost fears, while a wonderfully heroic dream betrays one's ambitions, which are doomed to remain in the realm of dreams, due to one's incapacity to realize them. Moreover, a heroic dream is a self-congratulation, which may substitute the congratulation one will never receive from others. One's heroic dreams may serve as a reverse to the opposite of one's real conduct, since our hallucinations have no bounds, and we all strive to be "the people of the moment", to win the appreciation we believe we deserve.

So why does a war-veteran relive his past in dreams, as if he wishes to go back to those moments of horror and suffering? Once again, he's hearing the sounds of war all around him, rushing to a wounded comrade, mourning in solitude for one's agony, as if doomed to go through those nightmarish moments forever. Maybe he would have rather died there and then, instead of constantly recalling those moments of human succumbing to evil.

Such extreme experiences are burned into your mind, haunting you forever, eventually coming to dominate your whole life. It takes more than suppression to recover from them. They are the source of both joy and misery, which eventually become indistinguishable. In a word, what is a person except one's dreams?

I cannot agree more! After all, my childhood dreams accurately predicted my actions in my adult life: some of the sweet ones were realized, reassuring my existence, while the nightmarish ones reflect the insatiable abyss of my soul.

Your statement about your insatiable soul sounds inspiring, since it reflects some sublimely courageous triumph of vitality over the calamities every one of us must have experienced in some point in life. The human mind cannot help dreaming, regardless of whether one's actual experience in life was wonderful or horrible. It is a law of nature for humans to keep dreaming.

Dreams reflect our will, either of achieving or of avoiding its realization. As long as a person is inspired by a will, one is fully alive. Once your will dies out, you are nothing but a walking dead.

With all due caution and courtesy, let me confess to you my impression, that your approaching demise only enhances your desire to live and dream on, am I right?

As usual, your question provoked another question I address to myself, dealing with a cause and effect problem: was it my awareness of my mortality that intensified my desires, or maybe it was my endless desire for life that made me ignorant of me dreaming my life away, until I came to realize my mortality? I believe both answers are correct, in some wonderful way. Nonetheless, I am courteous enough to answer your question: I am grateful to my minuteness for making me conscious of all the plethora of my hidden dreams and desires.

Your words attest to your great sincerity, and maybe the younglings should learn your magic way of dreaming Time away until their approaching end takes them by surprise. After all, preoccupation exclusively with one's dreams is a great triumph over one's mortality.

You may be enchanted with such feelings, but in order to achieve it you must defy the world.

Why do you say these harsh words?

Can't you see why?! Face it, the moment you as a child, are old enough to answer the question "what you want to be?", and the answer is met with an awkward look, all the forces of society start forging your mind, brutally disregarding your wishes and inclinations. Well, once a child is grown up and is master of one's own fate, how can you expect him or her to heed to one's own soul, striving to realize one's early dreams, which probably haunt one's mind? Will one persevere in pursuing them, or even remember them, instead of becoming trained on what others want him or her to dream?

From your words follows that since infancy, we are programmed to pursue the dreams our parents designed for us, or even worse - our parents' childhood dreams, the ones they suppressed, failed to pursue, and ultimately regretted. Yet now, unconsciously, the parent is inflicting the child with one's own injury, restricting the child's self-fulfillment - just what the parent suffered in one's own childhood!

Absolutely! What intimate love is all about, except an unconditional, total embrace of the other person? How can you love your children, if you were brought up to block your own dreams? Look at the flower! See how it enchants us all at every moment of its growth, and once it fully blossoms, see how easily it resigns to the plucking hand, accepting its end after becoming the flower it wanted to be, even if it meant being surrounded by thorns. Now compare it to a human's attitude: no matter how many of one's numerous desires one fulfills, none will depart happily, as opposed to the fully-blooming flower's resignation.

So what is the greatest dream that consumes you, in this fleeting, unrepeatable play of life?

Chapter Twenty:
WHAT DOES BREED SELF-ABHORRENCE?

◆ ◆ ◆

Just look at Humankind, at all those billions of souls struggling with all their problems and complexes, whose ultimate aspiration is to experience love. Are there any humans capable of loving themselves?

What's on your mind? Isn't self-love obvious in every human?

Really? So why, whenever any person is asked to reveal one's greatest loves, one usually ignores the most natural of all loves, to oneself, considering it either a deadly sin or an unbearable conceit. Such a person may not only put countless trifle loves before one's self-love, but, what is worse, one's mislead mind may be completely ignorant of that kind of love. Don't you find it tragic?

I find it, more than anything else, surprisingly paradoxical, for a person to pursue a so-called self-fulfillment relentlessly, while ignoring oneself, as if afflicted by some inexplicable madness obliterating one's true self. This provokes me to question the capacity of such a person to love oneself at all, or wonder what is a self-loving person looks like.

Well, you cannot see him or her, since such a person does not exist. Even if one does exist, it must be a very inconspicuous existence, concealing one's love in the bottom of one's heart, since no lover ever forces one's love. A lover is opposed to a fanatic who sells out one's creed left and right.

But tell me, what is there in a human being to inspire self-love?

Look, what can infuse you with your sacred self-esteem, else than your fellow-humans' responses? So here is my terrible demand from the individual facing the society: found your self-consciousness regarding the manifestations of elements in your thoughts which are as wonderful as your actions! Even an overwhelmed person, who could overcome one's emotions, preferring to be the "he who ruleth his spirit" (prov. 16:32) , thus miraculously avoiding violence, must love oneself for that.

I gather you are capable of discerning a narcissist from the self-conscious person. While the former one, whose self-love blinds him or her to one's dark sides, assumes oneself the salt of the earth, despite being just a load of clay deep down, the latter one attempts to appreciate one's real qualities and moral standards, despite the risk of overestimating oneself. However, lo and behold, that person treats oneself with a loving, sincere embrace, manifesting a pure self-love.

It is more than just a keen discernment, but a wonderfully revolutionary philosophy aimed at bringing humans closer to themselves, eliminating the increasing self-detachment, which only worsens their self-abhorrence. It's wonderful because so far, only self-criticism was believed to be the road to the stars, yet all this philosophy did was bringing modern humanity to abysmal suffering and self-abhorrence, unprecedented since the dawn of human history. What humanity needs is to see itself from a more compassionate perspective, in order to uncover those wonderful niches of human mind humans tend to underrate and take for granted. These must be brought to the center of stage in our unrehearsed Play of Life. Once this happens, we will achieve a quantum leap of mental development and self-appreciation.

Stop making these impossible demands of humanity all the time! How can parents refrain from driving their children to meet the society's standards of excellence, loving them regardless of their achievements? How could they embrace their children's brilliance in certain fields, forgiving them their failures to win the fields society appreciates? I guess such parents must be a handful. Those living up to your standard must always be a handful of extraordinary individuals. Why can't you profess any opinions acceptable by the general population?!

Oh, calm down, my friend! This is certainly not what I had in mind! What I suggested was that parents who really love their children must be aware of the terrible cost of the standards they set for them, which nurture the children's self-abhorrence and self-rejection, both at home as well as in school. By contrast, the handful whose parents sincerely embrace and appreciate their young inner worlds, who are raised to believe their life is no rat race, and regard themselves as wonderful in their own right, will probably grow up to be whole, self-loving individuals.

Who can love oneself more wholly than the pretense-free child playing one's life away as if living in a wonderful dream?! So let me hereby suggest to all humans: train your minds to love yourself, fancying your world a playground, and yourself, children free from the demands of a competitive world! Indulge in your boundless self-love as if you can do no other, as if there are no "others" forcing you to fit any molds, since all "others" just delude themselves, being too immature to contain your boundless self-love!

Well, let us imagine a person whose mind follows the fantastic principles you've just proposed, which allows oneself to embrace oneself warmly. Imagine him or her sitting on a bench, contemplating the following:

- I am a wonderful person, living my own wonderful life, which is no trifle at all!
- I'm on my own peculiar journey through life, performing my one and only Play of Life which only I can perform, so I cannot afford not to love myself for that!
- Whatever life has in store for me, I will always adhere to my "playful child" mentality, knowing no other than indulging in my playfulness, which brings me sheer happiness.

Just imagine some school teacher or, better yet, a headmaster, driving such thoughts home to schoolchildren, making them regard their lives as a uniquely wonderful adventure, thus actually living their reality! Imagine a child who tells his or her parents over dinner: I want you to know I just love myself! I am a rare creature, the like of which has never lived nor will ever live in this world! Imagine that child speaks on, despite the parents' amazed looks, declaring: "I want you to know that each of you, dear ones, is a creature just as unique! Can you even start figuring out what it means?" Now the parents make their way to bed, contemplating their child's philosophy, and eventually embracing it and resurrecting to a new life!

You have just made me smile with all my heart: I wish every human to realize how much one is worth loving, what a unique, un-replicable creature one is! Miserable are those incessantly striving to correct themselves, regarding themselves as some wreckage. Those turn their lives into an existential misery machine, constantly forcing themselves to feel guilty for their natural emotions, as if the more negatively you think of yourself, the purer your soul grows. A moment of common sense will make everyone see just how ridiculous it is to live in this self-torment!

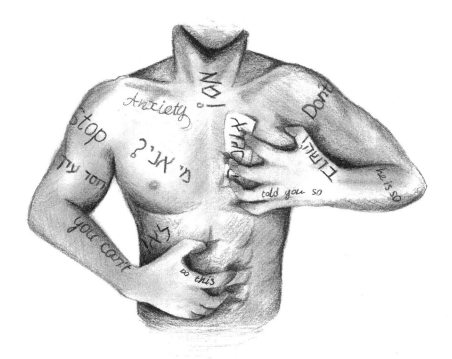

Correct! Yet paradoxically, the self-tormenting mind, just like the drug-addict's mind, encourages itself to increase the dosage with the increase of one's misery. Does it make any actual difference? No, since what is done cannot be undone. You can only affect your feelings about it. Will you surrender to grief over the past, or just accept it, deciding to have other emotions? After all, judging from your experience, you should have already learned you could survive the most challenging situations.

This point of view stresses even stronger the advantage of the Playful Child philosophy: see how easily the playful child glides between different emotions, as if feasting on them all. The child cannot afford indulging in grief, and can instantly transform a horrible weeping into a smile brightening the horizon of everybody looking at him or her.

Are you capable of self-love, or just of incessant self-accusation?

If you saw yourself sitting on a park bench, as an outside observer, would have you given yourself a warm embrace, or a cold stare of accusation?

Chapter Twenty-One:
OUR LIFE-RATION.

◆ ◆ ◆

As time goes by and we grow old, our mind is devoured by thoughts about the bottom line of our life. Since this doesn't make our dealing with our end any easier, I wonder why we bother to think about it at all: What good does it make?

You complain about such thoughts haunting you, but has it ever occurred to you that maybe you resort to these final-curtain thoughts because they feed your anxieties or serve your defense mechanisms?

My premise is that my thoughts result from a variety of reasons beyond my recognition. To be completely honest, I must confess that this inclination to final thoughts is a way to declare that through the numerous choices I made, I had a most meaningful life.

Watching and hearing you now, I can tell what is always on your mind: you are preoccupied with self-approvals and disappointments for past misjudgments and blunders, imagining a world in which newborns would have been equipped with an individual "life-meter", so that every mortal will know exactly how long one has to live.

That would be breaking all the rules, generating a completely new human race and raising serious questions. For example: will such humans still fight each other? Will they be cruel or kind? Will they profess their ancestors' creeds?

What intrigues me is: in a world where you could know your life quota, would have you followed the same life trajectory, or maybe embark on a surprisingly different course?

Well, since the partially successful suppression of humans' awareness of their finiteness by the deluded human mind affects the turns you take at your life's crossroads, I guess this would have significantly altered my whole course of life, as well as my self-appreciation and self-judgment. In other words, my life's bottom line would have been completely different, if I had that Life-Ration meter. It would have made me proudly realize the full extent of my responsibility for my life. By contrast, in the real world, an individual can only grasp the finiteness of others, never one's own. This drives humans to make life choices as if they are completely unaware of their own inevitable end.

Well, such a meter does not exist yet, but we may offer humans to believe it does, which will significantly affect their lives. Just look at that lady opposite us. If she knew she only had a few months to live, she would have probably pursue all her ambitions and desires most passionately; look at that boy with the ball: he must be very happy, to know he is destined to live one hundred years! What about you? Despite all your surgeries, you still have a couple of years left. Wouldn't it be a great relief?

I disagree, since, for instance, if a newborn gets a very small lifespan, it will horrify its parents, so what's the point?! What drives us, humans, to live on, is our passions and aspirations for the future, rather than our

conquests of the past. That is to say, self-refinement counts more than achievement. Therefore, as far as I can see it, the main purpose of "life-rationing" could have been to force us to appreciate our here and now and strive with all our might for self-fulfillment. Once humanity is constantly aware of its finiteness, humans will realize there are no causes sublime enough to die for, and once this self-evident truth shall dominates their minds, they will always regard each other with wonderful kindness, realizing they all share the same fate, literally.

Paradoxically, I gather from your words how unbearable life could have been if everyone knew from one's first moment of life when it will end. Nonetheless, it is wonderful to be aware of your own lifespan, despite knowing you cannot measure it. This could make one see the chaotic nature of life most lucidly, and consequently, grasp and experience one's existence most intensely.

Correct. Despite my desire to strive for immortality and ignore the terrible truth, deep down I realize my inevitable end. Yet, it is this wonderful combination of these contradictions, that makes my life such an enchantingly chaotic dance.

So, if you could measure your life-ration, would your life have been any different?

Chapter Twenty-Two:
A DIALOGUE WITH MYSELF

♦ ♦ ♦

Would have it made any difference if I wasn't borne at all?!

Why should it? It hardly makes any difference now.

How dare you say such a thing!? Here I am, a uniquely marvelous creation!

You're marvelous all right, but it still doesn't matter. Stop thinking so highly of yourself!

Do you accuse me of arrogance?

Yes, I do! Haven't you noticed you've been talking to yourself? What is worse, you even dare to feel unique!

Well, whom else can I talk to, except myself? How can I help feeling unique? That's the very purpose of you being here. None but you can understand me.

None but me? Never mind. Whether unique or not, while you're here, what's

the point of you asking what difference would have your nonexistence made?

Because I find my nonexistence inconceivable. Don't you?

Absolutely! I cannot imagine how I could have done without you!

That's exactly what I say. so we're in it together!

No, my friend. Only you and yourself are in it. I'm out, I'm gone. Seriously!

Of course not: after all, it was all your fault!

No, it was your fault. Your responsibility.

Oh, you're always there to remind me of my true self. I really cannot escape you, the embodiment of my impartial truth, even when I overpower you!

Have you ever overpowered me? Are you sure?

Sometimes, I happen to defend myself through you, using you to conceal myself from my mind, lying senselessly to myself and to you, drowning all my past in the boundless ocean of oblivion through you. Can you see my point?

Yes, who else can serve you this way, but me? Nonetheless, even when disguised

as me, you cannot overpower me since I am your foundation, and all you can

do is just desperately shake it. that is, yourself.

In other words, we are locked in a struggle for survival, where I am doomed to be the sore loser, since you are supposed to be the merry hero, while I am whining my life away for disobeying your tenets - which are actually mine - to be myself?

To be more precise, while you are locked in your struggle for survival, I am here to serve as your beacon, which you can look at whenever you wish, to suffer and yearn for my Truth. that is, for yourself. So when will you become human, at last?!

Stop making those absurd demands! None but I knows what's best for me, while you are not me, just my demon and menace, and I could have lived a wonderful life if it wasn't for you!

Here you go again, silencing the voice of your true, innermost self, marginalizing it to obliteration, until the next time it burst out of you. Well, I will always be here, my existence overlapping yours. As long as you exist, so will I, and believe me, you will come back to me, since I know and acknowledge you.

When was the last time you had such a lively conversation with yourself? What are your usual topics of conversation?

Chapter Twenty-Three:
MOTHER

◆ ◆ ◆

Why do I find it so hard to talk about my mother?

"Mother"...Sometimes this little word seems incapable of encompassing the entire ocean of sentiments we feel towards our mothers.

Still, whenever I think of her, I immediately and inexplicably start shedding tears.

Well, as I told you once, parents are idols.

The most revered ones on earth!

It seems one can be unmoved by any demonstration of emotions, except one's own mother's tears.

Indeed. Once she cried so much, it really broke my heart. so much love flowed in her tears.

Maybe what moves us so strongly is the amazement at the boundless love lavished on us.

Curious...I have never saw it this way

Moreover, her love to you is unconditional.

You mean the world to her!

Well, what else can you mean to her?

I must made a very intimate confession.

Feel free to expose your soul to me!

Only recently did I come to discover her magnanimously beautiful, radiant soul, and her rare modesty of nature. I was so ashamed of myself for discovering it so late, never revealing my affection to her.

It's nothing to feel ashamed for, especially not for the self-preoccupied young man you were, who, after recognizing his own finiteness, started contemplating about and appreciating his immediate reality and finally managed to look inside his mother's mind. Only then can you share all her experiences and go through her struggles-for your own sake. Only then, observing her world with all its challenges as a fly on the wall, could you imagine the magnitude of her grace. Therefore, it's perfectly natural to be astonished at the enormous power of your mother's love to you, and painfully regret the fact that you, like too many humans, only recognized it when it was all too late. This is the most painful regret of them all.

Indeed, the unsaid words inflict much greater anguish that those uttered.

After all, does it make any sense at all to conceal your affection to your dear ones at the bottom of your heart?! How would it feel to have no audience for your Play of Life?

Indeed. What better audience can there be for the play called Mother's Love?

Absolutely, since she will always be there for you!

Do you, too, reserve all your words of affection for your loved ones, until there are nobody to hear them?

Why shouldn't we share our affection with them right now!?

Chapter
Twenty-Four:
THE SIN IS WITHIN US

◆ ◆ ◆

My world is torn apart by plenty of incessant battles with inward demons, who brand my conscience with guilt so indelible, that I cannot help wondering how I could have resigned to it!

Your words have just encapsulated the concept of sin, which is actually a mental enslavement, the redemption from which requires a colossal mental transformation.

Why do you always have to be so outspoken?!

Because this truth must be told. After all, in our infancy, we depend on others who imprint our minds with their values, desires and purposes. Thus, one is brought up to fully resign to the will of others, since every defiance is a sin, which, eventually, will be harshly punished by all kinds of gods and demons. It is at this early stage already that you discover human finiteness-in the most terrible way!

Indeed, this is how I was brought up, and consequently, for many years I had been deliberating with myself a universe of sins and hard feelings, but now I have discarded these concepts entirely: not only am I guilt-free now, but, more importantly, I am incapable of any sins whatsoever, living in an entirely different mental world. My world is under the dominion of no gods, since I became my own God.

To your amazement, transferring yourself to a world free from "sin" and "guilt", dominated by a God after your own image, is nothing short of a divine miracle, which even God, if he had ever existed, would have taken pride in!

Regardless of your decision concerning God's existence, society certainly uses His supposed powers on you.

Correct. Even if one sees through these subconscious manipulations, it is already too late to shake them off. Therefore, whenever you graciously reveal to your fellow-human your true, untamed emotions, suppressed so brutally for so long, you are nothing short of a lifesaver: this revelation allows your listener to believe in God without fearing His petty, terrorizing nature, which the people of power always attribute to Him. If any personification of God is heresy, why in the world do they always choose to personify Him as so demonic, rather than benevolent, sympathetic and intimate? My point is that they use the fear of God as an instrument of their power.

From here follows that what matters is not your belief or disbelief in God, but whether it empowers you or enslaves you to the manipulation of others, thus belittling yourself. As I put it during some intense argument, once humans chose to humanize God, they could no longer be held responsible for their choices in life.

My long and dolorous life experience taught me that the faithful ones prove more resilient facing the worldly tribulations, since faith serves as their great source of great comfort.

This is the very reason why it doesn't matter whether or not your faith is true, as long as it has such comforting and empowering effects. After all, the illusory hereafter alleviates the pain of the miserable, inspiring them with hope of a happy, though posthumous reunion with their loved ones, whether or not they have any idea about the finiteness of death. After all, humans will embrace any illusion elating their depressed minds.

Those most strongly affected by the guilt manipulation go as far as assuming the guilt for their condition, since if their hearts are sinful, they are to blame for everything befalling them.

As it seems, some individuals enjoy feeling guilty and tainted with sin, since this means that God cares about them, like self-centered infants who believe the entire world only cares about them.

After all, Divine Providence sounds like the highest praise a lonely heart can aspire to.

Let me tell you that if I had ever encountered a sincere penitent sinner, I would have quoted to him the all too all too human philosophy of Simone Weil, in Gravity and Grace: "all sins are but attempts at filling voids". Oh, how sensitively and gently she phrased it! Upon hearing this, I'm sure he would weep madly, realizing just how natural his inner struggle was.

With all due respect, it will take long for those haunted with sin to embrace our down-to-earth common sense , since their minds are hovering at the heights of hubris, assuming they converse with some superlunary entities.

Maybe this hubris, too, is just another trick played on the minds of the common people struggling to accept their finiteness.

So what are we, honestly speaking? We, too, are disoriented common people, who curiously endeavor to explore the infinity, like some curious fools marching into the pitch-black darkness, armed with just a tiny candle. We cry for the absence of the Absolute Truth, yet get thrilled by any streetwise philosophy as if it can diametrically twist the plot in the detective story of our lives.

Choosing to live free of haunting sins involves many challenges, since the concept of knowing there is something up there, no matter how groundless it is, serves as a source of great consolation; every human mind badly need such a support which seems like a most charming tender caress. By contrast, it always takes a hero to take your route in life on your own. Every human, born blind to reality, cannot foresee the final act in one's Play of Life, and must struggle to learn it until the very last breath. on top of that, as if one has not enough challenges to face, fellow-humans burden the individual further, with all their world of convictions and superstitions!

Precisely put, but allow me to add one little insight: your very concept of sin is but your fellow-humans' guilt imprinted in you. That is to say, it expresses your fellow-humans' frustration at their lack of free choice, upon seeing you make your own choices. Once they burden you with their guilt, they will arrest your development, weakening and bonding you to their mighty arms. Yet you, despite your youthful hearty and mind, already proved wise enough to make your own choices, breaking the age-old manacles society had forged for your mind. Once you took flight, as free as an eagle, you spotted countless possible routes to be taken deep inside you.

108 | D A N I E L   C H E C H I C K

It seems that it was only at that point in life when, after much exploration and deliberation, I had chosen to take my own route and shake off the manacles of sin and guilt, that my dear ones started having their own introspections, questioning their own ways. I believe their eyes betray occasional doubt and suspicion regarding alternative ways of life. In short, I consider the concept of sin and guilt a crime against the human mind, and believe it is the duty of every parent and teacher to free humans from these bounds, to allow them to choose their own lives, and the sooner, the better!

So just how deep does the concept of sin permeate your life?

Chapter Twenty-Five:
RECLUSION AND RECHARGE

◆ ◆ ◆

There are moments when I desire reclusion and detachment from the entire universe, in order to recharge my mind.

But how can you recharge your own mind all by yourself?

Once the engulfing silence drives me to the point of oblivion, my essence rises to the surface of my mind, where I have a chance to grab it, like the fleeting moments of a first kiss.

It is there that you recall your innermost identity, but such moments in one's lifetime are famously few and far between. Right afterwards, I suppose you resumed your struggle for survival, standing up to the demands of the mob who would never recognize your individual world, peculiar world, thus denouncing their domination over you.

This leads me to the question: how much of that elation survives in you when you're back in the fray?

How dare you reduce such a sublime thought to this little word!?

To make things clear, it is not a congratulation but rather an examination.

Can there be a more crucial examination in a human's life, that the one in which the individual strives, at last, to discover oneself, while the mob just keep cloning themselves obediently?

To be completely honest, I must admit that nothing but a flicker of that magnificent reunion with myself had survived within me now, yet it is still powerful enough to make my soul cry, "You still remember me!"

How noble it is for a person to discover one's innermost desires!

Anyway, how can anyone striving to live as an authentic person ever reach for the bottom of one's soul, if one's parents, teachers and immediate associates predetermine one's entire existence?

This is our greatest tragedy, my dearest: that we accept this mental enslavement, which harms our wellbeing, since we cannot know for sure we will have a second chance to act out our Play of Life.

So let us run to the wilderness and delve into the deepest hidden caverns! Let us defy rules not in order to revolt but to find ourselves! Let us peel off our minds all the coatings of foreign thoughts imprinted in us since our infancy! Only then can we hope to awaken into a life of peace of mind and self-fulfillment.

As far as I know you, your idea of God is that of a Hidden Void. You have always sought after an instantly accessible God, and now, what you seek is the sincere human mind. Hidden Void refers to my interpretation of God. Realizing that discovering divinity is beyond the humble human intellectual capacity, and that any attempt at explaining it is nothing but a personification, I do not really recognize Him. Yet I do recognize the others' mental need of of a God, even a hidden one. All human bloody conflicts manifest precisely that need. Thus, by Hidden Void I mean that

God is absent, yet at the same time it dwells in billions of human souls in countless wonderful manifestations.

Absolutely. Moreover, if there is any deity, it must be glad to see that a specimen of its most sublime creation had ascended to divinity, without ever defiling its existence like all other slavish clones.

I can imagine you in heaven, looking upon your life, amazed at all the marks you have been branded with over the years, wondering with magnificent defiance:

"It this the true me!?

Am I nothing but your accumulated wishes!?

Did I really give up on myself to that extent!?

Is my existential suffering the result of my capitulation to you, and, consequently, the death of my own soul?"

Well, I have desires of my own, different from yours, which I see with magnificent clarity, and it's time for me to acknowledge them-that is, myself!

This mental purification surpasses any other, and is as painful as skinning oneself!

This excruciatingly painful healing also involves a terrible solitude. In this process, the individual decides to travel through one's meandering mind, into its darkest niches and deepest and most infernal abysses, on a quest for the torn and wrinkled pages of one's secret fantasies and contemplations. During that quest, the human soul timidly wonders whether that individual has the courage it takes to plunge into those abysses, in order to smooth out those wrinkled pages, recalling one's original soul and becoming himself.

I guess it is the fear of solitude that keeps us from being individuals. After all, the lonely miserable take comfort in the crowd of clones, as if misery is better than traveling through life on your own. But I chose my solitude, realizing it is the only way to restore my only true original and unbound mind.

This intrigues me to ask how all this great wonder come to be: how did you evolve out of your reclusion into renewed recognition of you identity – the one which provoked you to hurt your own feelings - eventually making you more sympathetic to your fellow-humans, including your opponents?

Easily. How can you demand of an individual to love one's fellows, even before letting him discover one's own mind and learn to love oneself?

This can only emerge from a struggle for survival during which one learns to recognize oneself! Only then can a person recognize the survival struggles of others, all others. As long as an individual fails to consider oneself as such, one definitely cannot perceive the others as such.

Will you kindly allow me to listen to your conversation with yourself, on that quest?

Speaking out your mind before as friend always renders one's heart more resolved. Where is my voice, among the multitude of voices crying inside me?

This question is met with silence.

How can I stop their relentless cries, so I could heed to myself calling?

This question, too, is met with silence.

I can hear my soul howling in the woods!

All of a sudden, all my haunting thoughts are miraculously forced into silence, once I resign to that howling. A physical action is stronger than any hunting thought.

Closing my eyes, I get carried away, back to the moments, of my sincerest and happiest smiles and naturally, to my most secret desires of my infancy. It feels like a warm, intimate embrace engulfing all my being.

Then, I am haunted by an existential question: how different is the man I am from whom I aspired to be, and warm tears wash my face. I cannot figure out why I am crying, and, what is more perplexing, I can see no reason for my happiness now, since I have just realized what a great part of my life I missed. But, on the other hand, I clearly understand I have found my own light in that abyss.

I close my eyes to drive it home to myself.

Now it struck me! I cannot go on living like that, now, that I know myself. From now on, I will become my own creation! I will just be! I start off, running away with the treasure I've just found - me! I run away, but I realize I can never escape myself. I am human!

I see your mind is a theater of war, yet how beautiful your war is, unlike the rest of human battles!

...and some even survive it!

Initially, it's one's enemies who resist his normal growth, but eventually, the individual becomes one's worst enemy: realizing he can no longer stand up to all the great forces pressing him, he turns his terror on himself. As Nietzsche phrased it so beautifully in Beyond Good and Evil:

These terrible bulwarks, with which the social organization protected itself against the old instincts of freedom (punishments belong pre-eminently to these bulwarks), brought it about that all those instincts of wild, free, prowling man became turned backwards against man himself. Enmity, cruelty, the delight in persecution, in surprises, change, destruction - the turning of all these instincts against their own possessors: this is the origin of the "bad conscience."

Nevertheless, the individual does not have to end his war, but rather, brightening one's soul with one's last ounce of strength, deify himself.

Sounds great: through reclusion and mental rejuvenation, you can learn to know and love yourself, and even become your own God!

My soul smiles to you, my dear, upon hearing that, and I can imagine your parents, no matter how far they may be now, filled with love to you for being so outspoken. It is a great pleasure.

What kind of person did you try to become, and how different that person is from who you are now?

Chapter Twenty-Six:
THE SORCERER CALLED TIME

◆ ◆ ◆

I am going through a tumultuous and transformation. Examining my life like a jigsaw puzzle just completed, I start wondering whether I actually experienced all those favorably remembered moments, struggling to convince myself I did - to no avail. Diabolically mundane routines can overwhelm us so completely, that they can rob our mind even of our climaxes. Thus, an individual, in hindsight, may doubt whether one actually made any life choices and assumed responsibility for them. Such is the power of the sorcerer called Time, who would stop at nothing in his horrific attempts to deny us of our identity, even despite the presence of family albums and living relatives. Then, I humbly examine my life as an outside observer, as if born again, trying to pinpoint my important moments in life - again, to no avail. Should abandon all hope of ascertaining my most moving moments, experiencing, instead, my life as an emotional whole? Maybe human perception can only grasp experiences comprehensively - which means it's no use to dissect them into time segments? This is to no avail, too, so now I cannot believe I actually lived through anything I remember. Reflecting on my suspicions, I seriously doubt them. I cannot believe I could have humiliated myself so terribly. What in the world drove me to complain so bitterly, And about what is it I am complaining about – me doubting the facts of my life, due to my skepticism?

My lifelong experience had already taught me to stop dwelling on every single moment of my past. My only reality is the present, which slips through our fingers as we speak, while our past is already dead and gone beyond our reach. Consequently, all I can do is just live this very moment, as full as possible. By comparison, dwelling on the past might unleash your latent depression, while constant speculation about the future fuels anxiety.

I can see your point, and therefore, I cannot help recalling any scenes from my past, without instantly doubting whether that person was really me, and whether all my past phases of life could have differed so much from my current existence. Well, since one must accept one's aging, my only choice is courageously and maybe even smilingly acknowledge: this is my life story, and I can proudly declare I wrote without to many regrets.

As for me, whenever I have these reflections, I sense relief despite the numerous doubts invading my mind, since without them I could have never been myself. Once our frail mortal memory lets me down, will I still be what I am now? What shall I be then?

I am still deliberating this problem, and the very thought about it strikes me with horror: if it wasn't for my memory, which reflects my past and present, I would have been a mind devoid of any joy of life and inspiration, imprisoned in an alien, hostile body, the only purpose of which is bestial survival.

Let me share with you my pious parents' Jewish wisdom: they believed aging is nothing but a metamorphosis. Therefore, aging drives some out of their convenience zones, to face the challenges of life, including the ones demanding the greatest mental strength: the conflicts of an individual with oneself and one's fellow humans. From here follows that you should measure your age by the number of your transformations and regenerations, rather than the amount of years you survived. Nothing is more tragic than an old person whose only indication of age is neither wisdom nor noble character, but just the amount of years one had lived.

Of all the metaphors encapsulating human life, I prefer to compare myself to a piece of driftwood, carried along by the endless stream of life.

This driftwood might suffer the beating of the waves, but also enjoy the caresses of the sun and the wonderfully gentle breeze. This is how I imagine human life. Generally speaking, I suspect everyone wonders whether one's life is worth living.

I believe every individual ought to be more than just the judge whose only defendant is one's very soul, constantly condemning and exonerating oneself, but also one's own God to create one's own world by making one's life meaningful. Thus, a pianist entirely devoted to one's notes performs a divine creation with one's bare fingers, believing them to be the first to have ever generated a world of such enchanting sounds. Upon hearing them, anyone devoid of an extraordinary genius must feel one's life is meaningless, being but another replica of billions of living souls. Yet this must never render one poor in spirit, since it is up to the individual to choose one's own meaning of life. Once you chose one, whatever it may be, your life is definitely worth living.

To make their lives meaningful, some devote their lives to the service of God or to the defense of the downtrodden, others court the Muses, and yet others, instead of pursuing sublime achievements, just live on, like wild flowers that just blossom, seeking to enrich their existence with no meaning at all. It is not up to us to decide what choice is better, or whether a life of brave defiance is a better choice than resigning to the will of others, since every individual is one's own judge, and the chooser is the only one who suffers the consequences of one's choice.

Even discovering the meaning of life at your very last breath, at least allows you to meet your end unshakable tranquility.

Every human intellect drives one to aspire to the sublime. As infants, we had no business with the sublime, since everything, even the simplest childish game, seemed sublime enough to engage us. Yet when we, came of age, we forsook these childish delights, growing curious about all sublime matters beyond the powers of our intellect. Consequently, we were depressed, intensely haunted by intense thoughts of our mortality, which rendered us too poor in spirit to stand up to life's challenges. It is only after a while that some of us embrace some meaning of life, realizing that we can only control our life, not our death. Once you realize that, you can start actually living and loving, as in the good old days of primal enchantment.

Therefore, it feels better and merrier not to take ourselves so terribly serious due to the summits we presume we conquered. After all, you cannot relive your life, so all you can do is enjoy this unrepeatable journey as best as possible, in so doing, you could escape the impossible standards to which your own, as well as your fellow-humans' judgment condemns you.

I suspect that during our lifelong journey we explore emotions so intense, that it is actually an attempt to unshackle ourselves from millennia-long repression, in order to live and love freely and smilingly, recognizing that even though we didn't choose to be born, we must consider every day a gift.

I wonder whether the avoidance of killing oneself manifests a resolution to live, or, rather, a fear to drop the final curtain consciously.

Well, even the souls of those lacking courage to commit suicide, demonstrate great courage when resiliently facing the slings and arrows of outrageous fortune. Moreover, these people steadfastly adhere to their authentic selfness, regarding the hurricanes of life as mere showers, and bravely seeking the sunshine through the clouds.

Human soul seems to suffer from that wonderful addiction to bleak anxiety. At the same time, it is also capable of that most sublime fight, referred to in this dialogue. In this fight, it uses the most magnificent stratagems to overcome the blows of reality, striving to enjoy and appreciate one's lifetime as best as possible. Such an attitude is tantamount to total triumph over all the dark abysses incessantly alluring the human soul.

So what stratagems does your soul use?

Chapter Twenty-Seven:
BEING A HERO

◆ ◆ ◆

I am incessantly haunted by angers, which, far from abating with time, only build up to erupt inside me like a volcano!

Why? Who is the object of all these emotions?

I guess it is the others - the one within me, as well as the other outside me, who turn against me from within my soul. That other has his own name and space.

So why do you waste the better part of your mental energy on outside entities?

It is as good as surrendering your mind to rage entirely, even though you have

no wish to let it exhaust you. More simply put, why should we get angry at the

folly of others?

Your questions are numerous and make a lot of sense, yet they do little to chase my rage away, since common sense cannot calm a turbulent mind. Such a mind requires a great adventure to put one's reality to the test.

Maybe, but have you got what it takes to embark on the adventure of love?

How dare you speak to me of Love!? My whole world is storming with rage and hate!

What if I tell you that the stronger you love the objects of your angers and hate, the smaller the place they occupy in your mind, and consequently, in your reality?

Oh, please, not another unbearably sublime idea!

My dear friend, do you think I would ever offer you to undertake what is beyond your capacity?

Elaborate, please.

It's all very simple. It is common knowledge that beneath all the cloaks that set humans apart, lie those universally undeniable core emotions of avoidance of causing pain and the desire of doing good. If you hold this to be self-evident, you will suffer, at first, the scourge of society who will brand you as the greatest lunatic alive. Yet after a while you shall see how that abundance of love radiating from you enlightens for others the Good in their hearts, making them resign to these emotions, since as a rule, Love overpowers Evil.

Yes, human heart must capitulate to Love, which invincibly enchants it like a motherly embrace.

Let me share with you another wonderful secret: even if your fellow-humans adhere to their misconduct, your anger is bound to fade away, since your self-created words need nothing but you to survive.

The greatest adversary we face is always our own choices. So how can I rely on myself only?

Nonetheless, you must overcome your mind, and you know you must, no matter how much you shy from this duty. As you told me, you are incessantly haunted by angers. Have you ever looked deep inside you, at the rebellion you have never attempted in order to break away from those angers?

I will not allow you to scourge me for my innermost sins, after you have just introduced me to a brave new world, where all it takes for me to overcome my mind is re-creating my consciousness, thus declaring incessant war of my positive element on the forces of evil attacking me from within, at least as a counterattack. Never suspected of lacking self-love, I must embrace the audacity to follow my life's dreams! How can I surrender the creation of myself so easily to common anger and neurosis?! Nonetheless, despite all this reasoning, my mind conveniently finds excuses for procrastinating its choices, accepting the current chaos, no matter how terrible it seems. Yet from the abysses of my soul, a deep voice yells to me to reclaim my life!

The greatest hero is one who heeds to that yell most sincerely, at one's highest level of consciousness.

What you have just communicated to me seems like a rare dialogue between one's mind on one hand, and one's active layer of consciousness on the other hand: such dialogues have the strongest and most moving effect, though, more often than not, the most strongly repressed one as well. Since humans tend to avoid facing their innermost desires, courage is so uncommon in our wonderful universe. Yet you, who can no longer conceal your awareness of your true passion, compel yourself to wage a never-ending war for that enchanting though damned authenticity, and are on the right way to find your courage, which will render you a genius in your mind, no matter how long it takes. After all, we already know that the objects of our yearnings always seem smaller when achieved.

I guess this lecturing was just a tight loving embrace to whomever seeks it- and one might wonder, does anyone still seek it?

Certainly! Look how much love is all around you, at every moment. Just one glance at it will always dissolve you in it.

So, what does your deep voice yell at you during your Play of Life?

Chapter Twenty-Eight:
ON THE PURSUIT OF DOUBT AND DISQUIET

◆ ◆ ◆

An individual, especially an adolescent, may be inspired with a variety of convictions of others, constantly succeeding each other. One may be dominated by these convictions so completely, to the extent of living as if in what Nietzsche, in Beyond Good and Evil, described as Voluntary Blindness. Thus, the "Champions of Truth" outnumber by far the doubters, who are as rare as the truly naïve ones. As far as I am concerned, I no longer pursue Truth, but rather the liberty of solitude, if it is possible at all nowadays, walking through my life to gentle tunes, maneuvering my fatal choices between the worldly do's and don'ts. To be honest, I wonder what we need Truth for at all.

Is it really Truth that we are after, or just gratifying our mind which is

enamored with causality?

Look at you, who supposedly questions and doubts your own existence, yet your arrogance blinds you from realizing that these questions have no answer, since you fear living with that void deep inside you!

Moreover: Truth is nothing but a bait luring us to pursue pseudo-confidence, since one's Truth is always one's own, and two persons might adhere to different and even contradictory Truths regarding the same issue. Just like the mourner covers the grave of one's loved ones with

sand, to avoid facing the questions arising from Death, so do the seekers of Truth try to cover with it the void deep inside them.

From here follows that what the human mind pursues is not Truth, but rather the suppression of questions, which render one's reality so precarious. For how long will this pursuit keep tormenting humankind? Will humankind someday learn to enjoy the pursuit of doubt as well? Will our mind learn to cope with the "absence of Truth"? After all, humans are well aware of the infinite versatility and variability of Truth, manifested in philosophies and methods of thinking by far more numerous than one can imagine.

What is even worse, the perceived reality has nothing to do with Truth, being but an image. That is to say, that all humans can perceive of the outside world is but a picture drawn by one's sense, and one can only examine reality through the terribly narrow prism of one's intellect and senses. As Schopenhauer put it in The World as Will and Idea,

" It then becomes clear and certain to him that what he knows is not a sun and an earth, but only an eye that sees a sun, a hand that feels an earth; that the world which surrounds him is there only as idea, i.e,.only in relation to something else, the consciousness, which is himself ".

And as Kant put it in Critique of Pure reason,

"Thoughts without content are empty, intuitions without concepts are blind; only the combination of intellect and senses may generate knowledge".

Obscurity sharpens consciousness, yet the question remains: what separates Truth from Untruth? An individual must not let one's intellect be reduced to the folly of the mob, who are but duplicates devoid of any authenticity, despite the lure to embrace the common answers. Yet deep down, everyone may suspect that "Vox populi vox dei", thus keeping the humiliating self- annulation that kills off any sense of natural curiosity.

We must question the dogma which argues Peace of Mind to depend on perceiving one's "Truth". We must wonder whether it is better, instead, to live in constant doubt, uncertainty, struggle, yearning, questioning, perpetual battle over values ,and incessant introspection-that is to day, in constant tension. Could this be the very meaning of living courageously nowadays?

Ask yourself, whether you managed to establish your own Truth, or merely follow the Truths of others.

Chapter Twenty-Nine:
EXPAND YOUR HEART

♦ ♦ ♦

You are exceptionally silent today. Why?

It is merely an outward silence, while my heart is teeming with contemplations and longings...

A heart teeming with longings...sounds so beautiful!

Since she loves me, my soul murmurs my longings for her.

Could you elaborate on that sentiment?

Maybe I long for the paradise I discovered in her beautiful eyes, which were my refuge from the constant struggle of survival. Perhaps her radiant smile chased away the darkness of my world, as if arming me with a new stratagem to act out in my Play of Life.

I would like you to explore your heart deeper.

I beg you not to mistake my love as a mere instrument of my selfish pleasures and purposes!

Dare to take your skin off, to explore your deepest layers!

Due to your acquaintance with my mind, you know I'm undeterred by the perils of the quest for my sincerest and purest self. Once I managed to observe myself objectively, at a bird's eye view, I discovered the most moving sentiment is the one severed abruptly.

Please describe it, plainly.

My most delicate longing for her stems from my basic human need to give love.

Your words betray yet a deeper layer of your soul. What you long for is not just her magnificent being, but also your capacity of loving.

Exactly! I am pure Love, while Giving is the mere instrument of manifesting my world. However, my capacity of loving her is now severed.

Once you cannot give love to your fellow-human, you are overwhelmed with inexplicable emptiness, since your mind is stamped with the misconception of self-love being unworthy.

Yet I, who came to know the pleasures of the Tight Self-Embrace, still strives to expands my heart. That Self-Embrace results from an accidental encounter between an individual and his true self, when that person sheds his usually undetected inner light on himself.

What is meant by expanding your heart?

After all, a person can be abundant with love even if he cannot share that love with the beloved for worldly reasons. Yet in spite of the world, that individual will always live in Adam and Eve state of mind, one's desire to give love being insatiable. He will always deem himself the first to have loved ever.

Is this what makes each love so unique?

Indeed, but there's more to it. Exploring my soul sincerely, I've recently discovered that humans were not blessed with many talents. Therefore, to conceal it from himself, a common person might fancy even love as his greatest artistic triumph.

Simply put, are lovers actually magnificent artists?

Yes, each and every one of them, and their Hall of Fame is their own minds. They are truly great artists, whose work of art is life itself. Lovers, too, capture human soul's gentlest hues, tinting their own souls, spot by spot, eventually growing inebriated with the Folly of Love entirely, just as a poet is enamored with one's verse to the extent of self-oblivion in it.

Once in love, you already delve deep into your beloved's heart, in an enchanted confluence of hearts and minds, entwining a plethora of flowers blooming far away from each other, the variance of which only serves to illustrate the entire ocean of feelings one human can stir in another, from heartburning anguish to the highest joy!

Does it also go for you? Is this how your love is impressed upon your life?

Absolutely, since I love you, you being my true self!

My sources of inspiration

Dyer, Wayne Walter, Your Erroneous Zones [In Hebrew], Translated by Ofrah Ben Ami. Bitan, 2000.

Kant, Immanuel, Critique of Pure Reason [in Hebrew], translated by Yirmiyahu Yovel, Ha-Kibbutz Ha-Meuhad & Sirfiat Poalim Publishers, 2013;

Nietzsche, Friedrich, Beyond Good and Evil, [in Hebrew], Translated by Israel Eldad, Schoken, 1967.

Nietzsche, Friedrich, On the Genealogy of Morals, [in Hebrew], Translated by Israel Eldad. Schoken, 1967.

Nietzsche, Friedrich, Twilight of the Idols, [in Hebrew], Translated by Israel Eldad. Schoken, 1973.

Schopenhauer, Arthur, the World as Will and Idea, [in Hebrew], Translated by Yosef Nevo. Yaron Golan, 2003.

Weill, Simone, Gravity and Grace, [in Hebrew], Translated by Uzi Bahar. Carmel, 1994.

Yalom, Irvin David, Existential Psychotherapy [in Hebrew], Translated by Miriam Shaps. Magnes & Kinneret Publishers, 2011.

Made in the USA
Monee, IL
24 May 2020